PRAISE FOR THE _CERTAINTY PRINCIPLE_

Robert Passikoff and Amy Shea, well known to us in the industry for their independent voice concerning brand measurement and effectiveness, have done it again! The Certainty Principle is a useful compendium of fact-based knowledge and strategic insights, wrapped in a readable and interesting framework. This book should be on every brand and marketing manager's desk.

Raymond Pettit, Ph.D., SVP, Research and Standards, The Advertising Research Foundation

Much has been written about engagement in communications but unfortunately the majority of this literature is either too vague or lacks application. The Certainty Principle stands apart providing a unique, well thought-out, and insightful perspective on how to embrace engagement – in all its flavors. For those who are involved in developing and evaluating communications this is a must read.

Simon Hough, Senior Campaign Insights Manager, Microsoft Corporation

Passikoff and Shea have written a really practical guide to measuring brand performance, backed by years of valuable, trail-blazing research.

Roderick White, Editor, *Admap*

Well-written and easy to read - a required reminder to the profession that effective advertising is not simply about entertainment - it has a job to do! Great lessons on how to achieve success in advertising and engagement with the brand in this complex media environment.

Abby Mehta, Senior Director, Global Marketing Research, Monster Worldwide

Passikoff's and Shea's true understanding of the differences between satisfaction and loyalty is what will make us all realize the full potential of our brands. This book explores beyond this world of satisfaction - the world of loyalty. In this world emotional fulfillment delivered by a brand or product can be measured within a competitive context to predict future business success. Shouldn't we all be interested in this?"
Kevin Kitagawa, Senior Vice President, Dentsu Latin America

The art of customer loyalty and brand differentiation is a learned skill. Only Robert Passikoff shows you how it's done in today's 24/7, multifaceted consumer world. With The Certainty Principle, your business will be unbeatable.
Farnoosh Torabi, Senior Correspondent, TheStreet. com TV and author of *You're So Money*.

If you've ever scratched your head wondering why some brands succeed and others fail, you need The Certainty Principle. Shea and Passikoff get to the heart of what drives consumers' loyalty to brands. Thoroughly engaging and at times humorous, their tales of how business leaders inadvertently overlook key drivers is akin to Jon Stewart's stories about the mishaps of government!
Leslie Zane, President, The Center for Emotional Marketing

Smart, savvy, and honest. If I were President, I'd nominate Robert Passikoff for Commerce Secretary because it would be nice for someone in Washington to understand what consumers really want. Buy the book, save the nation – and your brand.
Roxanne Roberts, Columnist, *The Washington Post*

Using Dr. Passikoff's approach we were able to identify elements of our content that truly connects our product with our audience. We used this information to repackage our product, placing more emphasis on content that emotionally engaged our audience and peeled away content that added less value. The result, we were able to strategically cut costs without damaging brand equity. Great stuff!

Karen Kokiko, Vice President of Marketing, *The Press-Enterprise*

Not every TV Rating is created equal. Take this book home and read it, so that next time your Media Director gives you the same old, well worn, media plan they have used for donkey's years, ask him which of those media channels will actually enhance brand engagement and loyalty by delivering increases in brand sales & revenue, rather than just measuring eyeballs and warm bodies for media impact allocations. Then next time, you may have a media plan that actually works.

Noel Gladstone, Vice President, Research & Development, MTV Networks, USA

Abundantly insightful and strategically sound, Shea demystifies what effective advertising is, and what drives it. If you are in the business of marketing or researching, your brands will benefit from The Certainty Principle's expertise and guidance. You must read this!

Amy Gantert, Consumer Research & Insights, US Smokeless Tobacco Brands

Robert Passikoff is a geneticist of sorts. He profoundly understands brand DNA: what makes a brand great, and what happens when just one gene mutates, for better or worse. To understand your brand – and the basic underpinnings of all successful brands – consider The Certainty Principle your textbook.

Lenore Skenazy, Syndicated Columnist

For those who really want to understand branding and how to integrate and leverage a brand into a successful marketing or communications program, this book is for you. Providing examples of many top brands miss the mark, it offers concrete and validated research-based solution designed to drive consumer action. Agencies, communications professionals, and research junkies who believe they know everything WILL learn something from The Certainty Principle!

Doug Turner, President, DW Turner, Inc.

Creative brilliance can steal 15 seconds of fame for your brand, but consumers engage only with compelling promises that meet an authentic need. The Certainty Principle is a call to action to enlist the consumer as co-creator of brand strategy, without whose active co-operation real brand engagement is not possible.

Dominic Carter, President, Carter Associates of Tokyo

Robert Passikoff is every marketers' 'go-to' guy for loyalty marketing. Nobody else has as firm a grip on the factors that cause consumers to feel a connection with brands – a responsibility that goes deeper than simply building brand awareness, trial and use. We ultimately must build deeper and more meaningful relationships with our customers. That is what Robert and his groundbreaking work on loyalty offers us – a means to build real connection with consumers.

Pamela N. Danziger, President, Unity Marketing and author of *Shopping: Why We Love It and How Retailers Can Create the Ultimate Customer Experience*

Certainty in predicting the outcome of major marketing investment is, seemingly, ever more elusive. Until, that is, the system outlined in The Certainty Principle, which helps brands actually predict profit delivery. For any CEO or Marketing Director operating in a brand-intensive marketplace not to consider this approach to marketing investment planning is just plain dumb, if not career compromising.

Kerry O'Connor, Business Enterprise Director; MGN limited, London

Call it brand psychotherapy. Dr. Robert Passikoff has been asking thousands of consumers for decades to talk about their favorite brands. The Certainty Principle has culled together years of insights to help marketers understand what engages consumers and drives behavior. Considering people's tastes can change faster than a teen can triple tap a text message, such bits of wisdom might just help keep marketers from going insane.

Kenneth Hein, News Editor, *Brandweek*

Robert Passikoff and Amy Shea have created a clear-cut roadmap for brands seeking the Holy Grail – engagement. The Certainty Principle is not theory, but a sure-fire, leading-indicator view of loyalty that works for any brand, in any category, anyplace in the world. Think of it as your GPS for engagement navigation.

Timothy R. Laurence, Ph.D., CEO, Richards Laurence Communications, Inc., Toronto, Canada

I picked up Robert's methodology at one company and brought it to another and I will most definitely take it again. It assists in taking the guesswork out of consumer marketing and does so with real-world results. A campaign launch with over 135% increase in sales did not come with luck but with great creative, messaging and a knowledge of what values and attributes were important to the prospective consumer.

Tracey L. Moses, Senior Director, Consumer Marketing & Worldwide Branding, Conceptus, Inc.

Until the day that industry creates a professional certification for Consumer Market Analyst, Robert Passikoff's work stands as the gold standard. Dr. Passikoff has an extraordinary ability to zero-in on those murky, oft changing emotional factors that drive consumer choice – and are 'make or break' for companies selling any product or service. The Certainty Principle's message is an invaluable sentinel for detecting the subtle shifts in consumers' mindset that soon will affect brands. Businesses ignore these sea changes at their peril. The American marketing landscape is littered with names of brands that did so and are dead or on life support.

Jim Ostroff, Associate Editor, Kiplinger Washington Editors

ALSO BY
__ROBERT PASSIKOFF__

Predicting Market Success: New Ways to Measure Customer Loyalty and Engage Consumers with Your Brand.

Student Attention: Measured by Photoanalysis

THE UNCERTAINTY PRINCIPLE

How to Guarantee Brand Profits
in the Consumer Engagement
Marketplace

Robert Passikoff, Ph.D.
Amy Shea

authorHOUSE®

AuthorHouse™
1663 Liberty Drive, Suite 200
Bloomington, IN 47403
www.authorhouse.com
Phone: 1-800-839-8640

First published by AuthorHouse 12/3/2008

ISBN: 978-1-4389-3542-3 (sc)
ISBN: 978-1-4389-3541-6 (hc)

Library of Congress Control Number: 2008910920

Printed in the United States of America
Bloomington, Indiana

This book is printed on acid-free paper.

DEDICATION

To our clients — the other believers — for
their great questions, what-if's, and wit.
And for feeding us occasionally. None of
this would exist without you.

CONTENTS

FOREWORD

One person with a belief is equal to a force of ninety-nine who have only interests.

John Stuart Mill

Bob Passikoff and Amy Shea are passionate believers about helping brands, and this book with its bold and honest assessment of the current brand, advertising and media landscape is proof. Brand Keys' clients literally bank on this validated methodology as a tool that inspires strategy; its uniqueness in a maelstrom of "useless" research product alternatives. . . none of which can hold a candle to it; and its infallibility as a predictor of marketplace success.

And, if you read it with an open mind, resisting the impulse to criticize it as self-serving because, by necessity, they cite the method, there is a .857 chance that you indeed will become a believer.

First, you have to believe that "brand engagement" is a proxy for brand sales. That's actually not so difficult. Brand Keys defines engagement as the consequence of any marketing or communications effort that results in an increased level of "brand equity." Brand Keys defines brand equity, very intelligently, as "the degree to which a brand is believed by the target audience to be able to meet or exceed the expectations the target consumer holds for the category in which the brand competes." A pretty neat definition, don't you think?

So, engagement is a marketing/advertising consequence that, in fact, increases consumer belief in a brand. Simple. Yet, metrics that can be said to truly measure engagement are not so simple to come by, especially those with the consistently high correlations to in-market and consumer behavior that abound in the Brand Keys case studies found in this book. Even if you do not get caught up in all the methodological details, the book will unequivocally prove to you that this is something you can use with confidence to successfully build your brand's sales.

So, buy the definitions, the fact that "belief" can be measured, and the .85+ correlations and you will become a believer, just like Bob and Amy.

And, if this book converts you, its value will easily exceed six figures on just the first brand that you turn Brand Keys loose on.

Good luck on your most pleasurable journey.

Robert L. Barocci
President & CEO and Believer*
The Advertising Research Foundation

October, 2008

We used Brand Keys to better understand the ARF brand. . . with great success!

__ACKNOWLEDGMENTS__

If, like Newton, we have seen a bit further about brands and engagement, it was not by standing on the shoulders of giants, but by leaning on the shoulders of the absolutely best collection of colleagues, advisers, helpers, and friends that the authors could have wished for.

They did not tell us how to write, but gave of themselves and their thoughts and expertise, and then left us to it. As such, this book would be incomplete without such an acknowledgment. And so, our thanks to:

Peter Boyko and Bill Callahan who have, for the past 25 years, allowed us to make the statement "the research goes out, and the research comes back," in complete confidence.

Dean Christopher, our Los Angeles GM, insightful brand strategist and our consummate scribe and craftsman.

Michael Lefkowitz, who manages the financial side of things and still finds time to clip articles that keep us up to date with the best data bases in the world.

Elise Passikoff, our Brand Keys web Mistress, for keeping us organized and readable.

Len Stein of Visibility Public Relations, the chief reason Brand Keys is the most quoted brand consultancy in the United States.

Gabriella Townsend, the "Voice of Brand Keys" and living proof that wonderful books aren't just written, they're copy-edited.

Jack Trout, the "Father of Positioning" and a fellow traveler in the fight against brand commoditization.

Alan Zwiebel, our creative guru, for always "putting his best man" on the job.

The Brand Keys team of Marilyn Davis, Leigh Benatar, Gary Anton Chalus, and Natalie Rosell Moreira who, once-again, are living proof that nothing is impossible if you don't actually have to do it yourself.

Our families, who heard all about this book for the past year, lived through our rants and re-writes, and never once told us to "shut up."

Lastly, the authors of this book would like to publicly thank each other for the intellectual engagement and boundless humor the other showed during the writing of this book, and throughout their partnership. And for never quitting research, at least not on the same day.

_____INTRODUCTION_____

What we need is not knowledge but certainty.

Bertrand Russell

Let's pretend you are Spain.

Brand Spain, being powerful and with the enviable ability to print money, has every method at its disposal to engage a potential traveler. It employs a media agency, and has skilled employees to manage that relationship. This team chooses the platforms and contexts that are best to communicate messages from the brand. These messages are created by an advertising agency, and include television, online, and even viral. They have been tested with a reputable advertising research firm. Brand Spain has also dedicated sizable resources to the creation of a positive experience with the brand, once the consumer chooses to interact.

Brand Spain, in fact, has spent a great deal of time and money on these methods, and in measuring their success or failure. It gathers data, and has very smart people to interpret these data.

What they are measuring against is what they have come to know about Brand Spain's previous and even potential customers, which is a great deal.

What they are *not* measuring is the consumer's "Ideal country" to visit. They are measuring Spain.

Of course, Brand Spain has some degree of engagement; many customers are loyal to Brand Spain. But Brand Spain would like higher levels of brand loyalty and more engagement with the brand because it wants more profits. So, Brand Spain examines everything that has happened, everything consumers say about why they chose Brand Spain — or why they are likely, having been tempted by the advertising, to choose Brand Spain next time. And Brand Spain keeps this information top-of-mind, as they use the old and new methods of outreach.

And they see small growth. They see that Brand France had a bit more growth; Brand Italy a bit less. They discuss why they think that happened. Strategies are tweaked.

And, while all this is happening, the consumer sleeps.

The consumer does not simply sleep, as we know, but also dreams. She wishes. She hopes.

She has, in her mind, an Ideal country to visit.

This Ideal is unconstrained by reality. It is perfection. It is a galaxy of emotion and experience.

Would you, Brand Spain, like to know what that dream is?

Would you, if you knew, be able to better strategize your media, message, and experience? Be more certain of your actions?

Would you, if you got closer to the Ideal, cause Brand France, Brand Italy, and Brand Greece to have long meetings about you, without refreshments, due naturally to the cutbacks?

Absolutely.

We look at brands from the desired result — consumer engagement — and deliver insights on how that engagement is created, as defined by the consumer's Ideal brand. Only then does the brand have a consequence-driven, consumer-generated target at which to aim their corporate and communications strategy.

Only then has Brand Spain measured consumers' engagement against what is *possible to own*, and not just present conditions. Because brands must discover what the consumer dreams of, not just what she sees.

This book is about a consumer view of the world of brands, and the evidence that supports it, because if there's any phrase being more widely-used in the world of marketing than "return-on-investment" (ROI), we haven't heard it. And rightfully so, with brands continuing to squander millions of dollars on low-return strategies and rudderless advertising campaigns. Procurement, as anyone in marketing knows, has found out where your desk is and wants an explanation for one of the largest line items on the corporate balance sheet. Validations and those pesky correlations to sales have raised their twin heads, and that is not going away.

Engagement has been a tough metric to define. The *Advertising Research Foundation* is already on definition 2.0, largely because the first pass lacked the concreteness that was corrected in the second. Having always put forth a behavior-centric view of engagement, based on something positive actually happening to the brand, we are delighted. There's a good reason, however, that a lot of smart folks have struggled with defining what we all agree is at the center of today's marketing paradigm.

Engagement with the brand is the ultimate objective. Nothing can substitute for it; nothing but that will ensure brand survival. Yet, to get there, brands need and employ outreach of all kinds — conversations, experiences, advertising, and every touch point possible and imagined. That outreach requires an engagement also. But it's not an engagement with the brand. It is an engagement with *the method* that the brand is using to get the consumer to engage with the brand.

There are four engagement methods but only one objective:

Methods:
1. Platform (TV; Online; Print; Sponsorship)
2. Context (Program; Webpage; Magazine; Game)
3. Message (Ad or Communication)
4. Experience (Store; Event)

Objective:

  1. Brand Engagement.

In a traditional scenario, a brand like Macy's might decide to use television (platform), buying time in a highly-viewed program (context) like *Heroes*, or running an ad (message) designed to bring someone into the store (experience). Each one of these methods is an opportunity to engage the consumer: television is a visual and highly-used platform, and "houses" shows that people are often connected with, and a good ad can peak interest in going to the store. Each one of these methods is also an opportunity for failure, of course. More and more people TiVo, or don't watch TV at all, preferring to catch their favorite programs online instead — absent the ads, naturally. And they can have a poor store experience.

This is an important point because, as you will read more than once in this book, getting attention and even awareness for a brand in no way leads *de facto* to engagement with the brand to a positive end. This can become fuzzy, especially as the scenarios become far less traditional than the one outlined above. Today, a brand may choose to host an extreme sports event, as Red Bull has done, with very little overt branding. Or a brand may recruit bloggers to try its products before a national release and spread the word, like Nintendo did with their Wii®, using blogs as the platform with consumer-crafted messaging — uncontrollable by the brand.

These, and hundreds of other forms of outreach, are being tried by marketers. With expanding technologies and opportunities for messaging, that's as it should be. What none of these scenarios should be confused with, however, is brand engagement.

Brand engagement is the consequence of any marketing or communication effort that results in an increased level of brand equity for the product/ service — and therefore loyalty, a leading-indicator of sales and profitability.

The ultimate objective of all outreach methods used by brands is the creation of brand loyalty. Brand loyalty is the reason for all media platforms. It is the reason for all contexts, such as television programs and magazines. It is the reason for all messages, commercials, and banner ads. It's the reason brands create a positive store experience or participate in an event.

Loyalty is generated when the brand meets or exceeds customer expectations in a particular category.

When a customer is loyal to a brand, he or she is engaged with that brand.

There is engagement that can happen when a consumer interacts with any of the methods brands use, certainly. That can and should be understood and measured; we are already measuring this, as the case studies in this book will reveal. But category and brand engagement, above all, must be measured. It is, in fact, the most critical measurement to take — and, most importantly, the *first measurement to take,* despite its position as the ultimate outcome of all the methods used by brands.

It is a logical question to ask how one would measure an end result before methods to accomplish that result are employed.

The answer is that one must measure the Ideal end result, using metrics designed to predict consumer behavior.

Remember Brand Spain? This book will demonstrate how measuring the consumer Ideal in a category is the most valuable benchmark you can have — far exceeding any average of past performance, no matter how specific. Once you know the Ideal, you can measure anything against it: a brand, a brand in combination with various media platforms, programs or touch points, and any brand communication.

The Ideal is the consumers' view of the world of brands, as this book will show. And measuring the Ideal, and the brands against that category Ideal, is predictive of consumer behavior *before* it shows up in the marketplace.

To support this, we have included excerpts from our own blog, The Keyhole (http://brandkeys.blogspot.com/) that we have written since 2006, inserted at the end of every chapter. Please note the dates. As well as reinforcing insights with concrete, real-world examples, we believe they help demonstrate that our data gave us information about category activity and brand performance long before the press began to report it. We've appended each excerpt with subsequent media reports on brand marketplace realities — our blogs ranging from 9 months and 10 days all the way to 2 years and 7 months ahead of marketplace realities. The case history about Starbucks' ascension and decline, included in this book, is a concrete example of the predictive nature of the data.

This book, ultimately, is like our model: results and output focused. In times of big changes especially, theories abound. While theories are the foundation of any good research question, they are not a deliverable. They are especially not a deliverable when brands are struggling for research applications that can help them face the future with greater certainty.

While the case studies in this book focus on big brands that are familiar to us all, any brand of any size can create engagement. "Fred's Breakfast" in New Hope, Pennsylvania, with its membership-only customer base, went far beyond a mere gimmick in approaching consumers. Customization of the dining experience via design-it-yourself membership applications that resulted in literally the shirt off the back of one applicant and the back of a competitor's breakfast menu from another, and a strictly word-of-mouth campaign, was at the core of the brand's appeal (along with a great breakfast). It thrives as a result. Fred's did not copy but instead it invented, looking beyond the common to the ideal community breakfast spot. While it will never be a large-scale threat to McDonald's, in New Hope at least, neither the golden arches nor local competitors stand a chance against levels of engagement like that!

Any brand, no matter the size, can profit from understanding the central principal behind the stories in this book: that only a deep understanding of what creates customer loyalty and engagement will take brands into the future. Innovation — whether technical or theoretical — is far easier to support and manage when the brand knows with absolute certainty what is important to the consumer, and where it will get the most return.

Technology — as a platform and as a diagnostic tool — is not the 21st century's "silver bullet" either. We are in a time of tremendous advances in understanding how we humans think. Neuroscience has already entered the field of <u>marketing research</u>, and continues to refine its often-clumsy and intrusive testing processes to get a piece of the research pie. The methodology that can crack the code of the human mind will still have one major obstacle to overcome — it will still have to give its subjects something to respond to, which means, by extension, something which already exists. Brands that face the constant challenge of taking their charge in new directions, often find this prospect less than satisfying. They need to answer major strategic questions of allocation of resources for product development, media, and advertising creation. What part of the brain that responds to a logo or, with greater specificity, responds to particular images, does not help a brand to know necessarily what direction is the best one to choose.

Communications research especially operates in a stadium where the rules change depending on what team you are on. There are many methodologies out there from good people trying hard to discern how the "stuff" brands say is received. Some of those testing systems have been around for a long time, and some have even developed very good methods of understanding executions. But they lack a strategic view of the brand. Not designed to offer a benchmark beyond previous performance of advertising (hopefully at least in-category advertising), the question of whether an ad is "good" or not often goes unanswered. Yes, it may do well in the testing and even win at awards shows. But in terms of whether it is performing against a consumer-based category-centric strategy or not, that is not a question that copy-testing can accurately answer. To answer the question "Is this a good ad?" you need to know what you were trying to do in the first place.

And for our tastes, there are far too many brands out there with so much at risk, that cannot answer that question. Whether for communications, development, or resource allocation, only knowing what you are trying to do will take you there.

And the answer to how you know, with absolute certainty, is where this book begins.

1

Twenty Absolutely Certain Things about Loyalty and Engagement

The race is not always to the swift nor the battle to the strong – but that's the way to bet it.

Damon Runyon

The typical gambler might not really understand the probabilistic nuances of cards or dice, but when it comes to betting, such things seem less complicated when compared to branding and marketing in the 21st century.

Dealing with consumers, who more and more have the power to block carefully crafted communications, is making things difficult, to say the least. Recognizing that they can exclude you from their 24/7/365 online, socially-networked blogosphere conversations is exasperating. Navigating a more and more complex multi-media multi-platform multi-marketing environment is both bewildering *and* frustrating. Brand differentiation is more and more difficult to both attain and retain. The convergence of — and the conflict between — many aspects of modern life and technology has resulted in more and more unanticipated and revolutionary market transformations. And, as C-suites and shareholders demand greater levels of accountability — don't you wish you had a dollar for every time you've heard the term return-on-investment (ROI)? — more and more marketers end up betting their brands' futures based on data from assessment techniques that were outdated nearly two decades ago, keeping more than a few folks up at night.

We continue to hear at conferences how measurements are lagging behind the realities of today's rearranged world, but that simply isn't true. Real loyalty and engagement metrics are available and have validations enviable by any standards. The metrics described here and in our first book, *Predicting Market Success: New Ways to Measure Customer Loyalty and Engage Consumers with Your Brand*, can help even out the odds for marketers. Think of it as a kind of anti-business-as-usual approach for marketing folks not bound to conventional ways of thinking about customers, brands, markets, media, and the assessment of those critical marketing aspects.

Since the publication of our first book, we have continued to adapt our metrics to the increased demands of an already-challenged marketplace. We've applied them to identifying real engagement and uncovering real opportunities for brand differentiation, as well as creative assessment and media optimization. We've found that real loyalty and engagement assessments can indeed measure integrated communications and can predict the outcomes of blending platforms. This approach has continued to identify trends that virtually guarantee brand engagement. It's been tested and re-tested and it always proves out in the real marketplace. Always. There aren't many systems that can say – or prove – that statement.

As a preamble to the actual studies and solutions, we offer twenty absolutely certain things about loyalty and engagement — the way to bet if you want to win.

1. Consumer behavior and engagement can be predictively measured using loyalty metrics.

Yes, it takes some thought and design skill, but virtually any aspect of the marketing mix can be measured predictively. These metrics are quantitative and generalizable at the 95 percent confidence level. They can be applied to brands, categories, or audience segments. They can measure communication, promotions, sponsorships, and media — and they increase your odds of winning. Always.

2. Awareness is not loyalty. Awareness is not engagement.

Everybody's heard of General Motors, but compared to Toyota, fewer are buying their cars. Everybody knows the Gap, but their same-store sales have been in a death spiral for years now. "Awareness" is an easy metric to measure and understand, but it is the longest route to profitability you can take and it has absolutely nothing to do with loyalty or brand engagement.

Awareness is being quoted so often as an indicator of, or absolute proof of, engagement that it has started showing up printed on refrigerator magnets in marketing conference goody bags. It's a popular fall-back, largely because it's easy to measure, but it is neither a measure of consumer loyalty nor brand engagement.

3. *Loyalty is a leading indicator of positive consumer behavior and profitability. It is predictive of what will happen. Always.*

A leading indicator is a measure that changes before a market metric, *i.e.,* customer sales, has changed. Our loyalty metrics indicate change about 12 to 18 months before marketers see such changes reflected in consumer behaviors, sales, or profitability. Leading indicator metrics show up well before inklings of such changes are articulated in focus group discussions or show up, if they even do, in traditional tracking studies. And, barring egregious corporate mismanagement, they correlate with how well a company will do financially. Always.

In 2005, Aquetong Capital Advisors, a leader in corporate valuation, wished to add loyalty and engagement metrics to their traditional assessments and examined the correlation between Brand Keys loyalty metrics and their company valuations. Without our input, they selected ten categories from our *Customer Loyalty*

Engagement Index®, and conducted correlations against our loyalty rankings. The correlations between the *Customer Loyalty Engagement Index* assessments and their financial assessments ranged from a low of 0.83 to a high of 0.901, which absolutely confirms the ability of a loyalty-based system to correlate with positive and profitable behavior toward the brand. We welcome you to visit our website (www.brandkeys.com) where annual brand loyalty rankings are posted and you can conduct your own analyses.

4. Satisfaction is not loyalty.

No matter how many marketers and conference coordinators lump them together, loyalty and satisfaction are not the same thing!

Not long ago, say 1960 to 1985, companies didn't really care if customers were satisfied. Think back to what your bank was like. No free checking (likely no free anything) and if you didn't like it, well, there was the door — oh, and by the way, we'd like our toaster back. So, as rational differentiation became harder to come by, companies decided that it might actually set them apart if they satisfied customers. The economics of customer loyalty were still important, even if marketers weren't paying attention to that aspect of their business, but most companies had to actually learn how to satisfy customers. Enter the Customer Satisfaction Movement.

Quality wasn't job #1 for lots of companies back then either, but someone discovered that the products and services doing what they said they were going to do had become more critical to financial success. Door handles shouldn't fall off new cars as they were driven off the lot. Clothing and bedding shouldn't disintegrate in the washer or dryer. "Twenty-four hour delivery" meant getting what you expected in a day, not a week. Problem resolution should be now, not later. Things like that actually had to be learned too, which delivered to the marketplace the newest initiative of the year: the Total Quality Movement. Once everyone managed to do all those things, the products and services turned out mostly "right" and pretty much the same. The age of brand ubiquity had begun. And nearly every brand "satisfied" customers.

Today, satisfaction is "table stakes" (or should be). You either have it or you don't even get to play in the category in which you compete. At any rate, you don't get to compete for long. Today, satisfaction is a 'given' and you either have it or you die.

While marketers find some small comfort in understanding how satisfied their customers are, and think it conveys some level of brand differentiation by mentioning it in their advertising and on their websites, they ignore the fact that satisfaction measures are "lagging indicators." A lagging indicator is an economic indicator that reacts very very slowly to economic changes, and therefore has little predictive value. Generally, these types of indicators follow an event. They're what happened the *last* time. They're a backward view and are historical in nature. If you need a more visual image of the difference between satisfaction and loyalty and the inherent danger of confusing the two, think about driving down the Interstate at 75 miles an hour using only your rear view mirror to steer.

It's worth remembering that two million iPhone® owners were once someone's "satisfied" customers.

5. *Loyal customers are profitable customers.*

Yes, there are lots of ways to segment customers. The current rage for database research, where credit card and customer loyalty program data is crunched to deliver even more information on what current customers did last time, surely delivers more data than can be shaped into increasingly niche customer groups. While there are no doubt some interesting factoids that emerge from that type of analysis, perhaps even helping to mold inventory and couponing programs, these micro segments are often "unbuyable" from a media perspective. All that aside, the kind of strategic boldness that brands need to excel will only come from examining *how* consumers buy, not *what* customers bought.

Naturally, there are some loyalty segments where you won't make as much money as you'd like, but identifying customers on that basis requires a fairly sophisticated economic analysis. You'll be ahead of your competition if you get the basics right first. Generally speaking, it's fair to say that it costs substantively more to bring in a new customer than it does to keep an old customer, and your profits will increase as your loyalty bonds intensify.

There is, however, a fairly simple way of understanding the overall rewards of real loyalty. It's called "The Rule of Six" and to illustrate each, we've put it into the context of an individual brand that receives exceptionally high loyalty ratings.

It goes like this: Loyal customers are six times more likely to:

- Buy your products (7 out of every 10 MP3 players sold are Apple),

- Buy more of your products more often (92% of Apple iPhone users also own iPods®),

- Recommend your products to friends and family (Apple's top-2 box "willingness to recommend" has increased by 20% over the past 18 months),

- Invest in publicly traded companies (At the time of publication Apple has had a 52-week high of $202.96 a share),

- Rebuff competitive offers, especially price-based offers (see previous four points), and

- Give your company or brand the benefit of the doubt in tough circumstances.

It's also worth remembering that the Tylenol brand went through seven rounds of poisonings and the brand came out more robust every time. Yes, Tylenol handled the PR just right, but they survived primarily because customers were loyal to the brand.

If you want a more contemporary example of how important getting the benefit of the doubt is these days just think about Apple and AT&T.

Since the debut of the iPhone 3G in July 2008, buyers loudly complained about poor network connections and dropped calls. These days, consumers don't expect that to happen. The loyalty driver "Clear and Uninterrupted Calls and Connections" accounts for nearly a third of the engagement and loyalty bond in the Wireless Carrier category. With nearly 90 percent of the population already owning a cell phone, there's little room to grow, so loyalty is more important than ever.

At the time AT&T offered the iPhone exclusively, so they received the brunt of the complaints regarding problems with their cellular network. AT&T's competitors had a field day exploiting that situation with full-page ads that read, "A phone is only as good as the network it's on."

Unfortunately for AT&T, that's a statement consumers were willing to believe, because while fingers were pointed at both the phone *and* the network, iPhone owners were generally forgiving of Apple, not an entirely unexpected reaction. Loyalty ratings and consumers' emotional bonds were – and remain – very, very high for Apple, whereas they were not as high for AT&T. And, as the "Rule of Six" states, where loyalty is high it's pretty certain that you'll be the brand that gets the benefit of the doubt in tough circumstances. And, unfortunately for wireless carriers with lower loyalty levels, when the going gets tough, the tough move their accounts to other networks.

6. *The decision process — whether Business-to-Business (B2B) or Business-to-Consumer (B2C) — is more emotional than it is rational. Most assessment systems don't truly account for the emotional aspects.*

In 1997, Brand Keys introduced the *Customer Loyalty Engagement Index.* Eleven years later it examines 57 categories and nearly 500 brands. The output of the loyalty assessments identifies the drivers of engagement and loyalty. In 2005, we conducted an analysis examining what really drove the decision process. We discovered that the consumer decision process was more emotional than it was rational, and unless you were a commodity, it was true in all categories. At that time, we identified the ratio at 70:30. Since then, others echoed our discovery. Some say the ratio is 75:25 and some say 85:15, and yes, it varies slightly from category-to-category, but it is not 50:50.

The 30 percent that's rational is mostly an aggregation of what marketers and marketing textbooks refer to as "The Four P's." The 4-P's refer to the *Product* (the stuff or service being sold), *Price* (the cost of the stuff being sold), *Place* (where and how the stuff is distributed) and *Promotion* (marketing, advertising, promotion, and engagement programs for the stuff). The philosophy in the early days of marketing, nearly 60 years ago, was that the brand that was best able to manipulate the 4-P's would be the winner. And it worked — for a time — when customers were far less sophisticated and brands were far more differentiated. Don't misunderstand us. Rational aspects *can* differentiate your product or service *if* there are real differences. For example, according to full-page newspaper ads, Campbell's Select Harvest® soups "never add artificial flavors or MSG" while Progresso®, the ad infers, does. This may be a very leveragable, rational differentiator *if* the lack of Monosodium Glutamate is an important contributor to category engagement. Real engagement metrics can tell you whether that's the case or whether you are just talking to yourself.

But today, that 30 percent is rational, undifferentiated, and generally *not* a high contributor to engagement and loyalty. Pick any brand in trouble and run it through the list, those rare examples of true primacy of product or service notwithstanding, and you'll find that every company and every brand that managed to survive into the 21st century is doing the 4-P's right — and pretty much the same. GM? The cars are as good as their competitors. Really. Ford too. Recently, Ford took the nameplates off their cars and traded them with competitive brands that the customer had just bought. The result? Well, in the commercials anyway, all the drivers who had purchased a competitive brand were ecstatic about the Ford, or, at least the unbranded car they had been driving for the past week. What it proves is that the product was as good — maybe they thought it was even better — than the automotive brand they had purchased. Was there anyone who hadn't heard of Ford? Did they not know that there was a Ford dealership across the street from the Toyota lot where they actually bought a car? And was the pricing so significantly different that they couldn't help but buy something other than a Ford? No, we didn't think so either.

So if all the "rational" 4-P's part of the equation are equal, what ultimately drove the final decision? What remains of the decision process that marketers should be looking to control? The answer: all the emotional elements. But, there's a difficulty in moving marketers away from the rational 30 percent and getting them to concentrate on the emotional 70 percent because marketers and brand managers find the 4-P's model comfortable. It's easily understood because it is one of the legacy measures that's been around since 1954. As one senior brand manager at a Fortune 500 company put it, it's something we can "get our heads around."

But as more and more of the decision process migrates to an emotional basis, and as more and more CEOs, CFOs, and shareholders ask, "What are we getting for our efforts?" marketers will have to start getting their "heads around" emotional engagement metrics.

And when they finally do, they will need to be wary. Don't just nod your head when the agency or consultant tells you something is "emotionally-based," or that a metric will identify the "emotional bond," or such-and-such will measure "emotional engagement." Ask, "how and where and what will I really get? How is that 'emotional'?" You deserve a response that makes sense, or all you'll end up with are excellent answers to meaningless questions. You'll have data, but you won't have emotional insights. Emotional measures *absolutely must* get below the excellent radar of consumers' "thinking" response.

And if you think bad measurement just doesn't happen these days, that researchers have become smart about this stuff, here's proof that the hard questions need to be asked—and not of respondents, but of the research team.

Heard of *Harry Potter*? Think kids have heard of Harry, Ron, and Hermione and maybe have some interest in them, interest that may have even increased as the books were released? Do you then think that these same kids, talking to each other say, *it was so cool when Harry got the snitch, though, Bobbie, I sometimes wonder, is Harry a fading phenomenon?*

The obvious fact that kids don't talk this way apparently eluded brand consultant, Martin Lindstrom, who, along with research supplier Millward Brown conducted a study that resulted in the following statement: "*Harry Potter* is headline news today because of the media blitz surrounding the new (6th) book. Six weeks later you won't hear anything."

This declaration was based on an 18-country study where children, seven to twelve years of age were asked, "whether they thought *Harry Potter* was a fading phenomenon." Mr. Lindstrom reported 69 percent said "they did" and, at the time of his interview, it was now "probably closer to 80 percent."

Reading this we had four reactions:
1) Are you crazy?
2) Boy, I'm glad I didn't pay for that research, and
3) What a muggle!

Our fourth reaction has to do with the fact that maybe direct, rational Q&A isn't the way to go when measuring emotional engagement with a cultural tornado like *Harry Potter*. The emotional bond to the character (and the books, the movies, and the licensed merchandise) had to have been something more than a rational reaction like "boy, that's a good story and 600+ pages for $19.95 is a good value!" or "I've got nothing to do. Let's go to the movies." Really.

But let's start with what was asked. Did 7 year-olds even know what a "phenomenon" was? Did the researchers consider what the category drivers were for the category and how people — children especially — were engaged? People rarely think about a book or movie until just before its release, particularly children who are generally "of the moment." Did the researchers consider a more behaviorally-configured question like "Will you or your parents buy the next *Harry Potter* book (or see the next *Harry Potter* movie)?"

Direct and rational Q&A may get you excellent answers to meaningless questions, but being able to truly assess the emotional elements of your brand or creative can be sheer magic in the marketplace. Just ask J.K. Rowling.

7. *You need to examine your category through a consumer lens.*

Yes, you know your *category,* but you can't possibly view it in the same way as the customer, no matter how hard you try and no matter how many ethnographic reports you read. You are always going to be too close to it and will nearly always base decision-making and identification of insights on/from the brand's perspective.

The Brand Perspective is

- Organized,

- Product-Focused, and

- Siloed

The Consumer Perspective, on the other hand, is

- Over-Messaged,

- Solution-Focused, and

- Viral

And while "consumer perspectives," "the voice of the consumer," and "consumer generated insights" have been the catchphrases of the past decade, if you look real closely, you'll find that your direct Q&A, your conjoint analyses, your demographic code-and-tabs are providing rational — not emotional — insights.

8. To have real predictive loyalty and engagement metrics you need to "fuse" emotional and rational aspects of the category.

That's what Brand Keys does. Our process is based on identifying the emotional factors and fusing them with rational category attributes, benefits, and values (ABVs).

Our questionnaire "fuses" emotional and rational values that govern brand engagement and loyalty via a combination of indirect, Jungian-based psychological inquiry and higher-order statistical assessments including factor, regression, and causal path analyses. The questionnaire has a test/re-test reliability of .93 off National Probability Samples in the US and UK and has been used in B2B and B2C brand strategy and media scenarios in 27 countries.

As supported by both the scientific and the research community in its study of emotional response, questioning someone directly about emotions very often leaves the most important things unsaid. Few, if any, middle-aged men will tell you they bought their red Porsche as a container for their Viagra, and a way to get them to need it. They will talk a great deal about superior design and high speed—the more rational reasons that do not help a marketer very much.

At a recent research conference, a presentation on emotional icons and their ability to diagnose advertising response was so obviously inadequate that the audience began to chuckle. An overtly-sexual ad for cinnamon chewing gum, featuring a teenage boy on a couch sandwiched between his date and his date's very hot mother, clearly not watching the TV screen, was analyzed as an ad that respondents emotionally identified as "happy." These are the kinds of findings that spread the ugly rumor that emotional response is un-measurable—a statement patently untrue.

9. *Real engagement and loyalty metrics are bulletproof. And validated.*

It is eminently possible for reality to triumph over skepticism, particularly when you have the proof to back up what you say. The Brand Keys methodology that you'll see reflected in the following chapters has been vetted via the *Advertising Research Foundation's* First Opinion Review. (Feel free to download a copy from our website.)

That said, except where we discuss "process," evaluations and commentary are backed up with real-world cases in point and actual in-market validity studies. In every instance you can see what engagement and loyalty assessments predicted (AKA, what *should* happen), and compare that with real market activity (AKA, what *did* happen). We are extraordinarily proud of the fact that Brand Keys has more validity studies than any other company claiming to provide similar assessments and insights.

As we continue to match our loyalty and engagement assessments to the demands of the 21st century marketplace, we regularly publish articles and share these insights with our colleagues at a number of forums annually. We urge you to ask your agencies and suppliers if they can show you *how* their data predicted what actually happened in the marketplace. Did they know what was going to happen, or is this just another chapter you can add to your brand's marketing history?

10. Consumers use the Category Ideal as their "yardstick." You should too.

As any good marketer knows, consumers do not buy colas the way they buy cell phones. And, in spite of the fact that consumers don't buy wireless they way they buy bottled water, a good many suppliers and agencies trade away product and category specificity for cross-category generalities. This may be helpful in creating averages, but has nothing to do with how people actually behave — "behave" being the operative word, especially when you want engagement and loyalty metrics that actually predict what is going to happen when you spend your multi-million dollar marketing budgets. As such, we use the Category Ideal and identify it via our emotional metrics.

Creating an ideal is a natural process based on experience, desire, knowledge, and expectations — four very different aspects that can neither be fully described in direct language nor accurately measured on sets of scales. This is why, once again, indirect emotional measures are so critical in assessing engagement and loyalty. You must do that because having consumers overtly "Rate the Ideal" via importance scales may make for an unobjectionable cable reality TV concept, but it makes for a lousy marketplace yardstick.

11. Loyalty and engagement assessments should be easily understood and should not look like EEG charts or mutated quadrant maps. (Also, they are not static like the Elgin Marbles either.)

All of the output that accompanies cited studies is expressed as easy-to-read diagnostic bar charts or overall index numbers.

Each product category Ideal is described in four bars representing the category drivers. They are listed from left to right in order of their importance to the customer in the engagement-loyalty-purchase process. They describe precisely how the consumer *views* the category, how they will *compare* offerings in the category, and how, ultimately, they will *engage and remain loyal.* Sometimes you'll hear that described as how the consumer "bonds" to the category or the "emotional bond" between the consumer and the brand. But saying it and measuring it are, alas, two different things. The causal path analysis provides the percent-contribution each driver makes to the engagement and loyalty process, which can be helpful in brand planning or in making strategic brand investments.

Figure 1.1
Sample of Data Output: The Category Ideal
Wireless Carriers

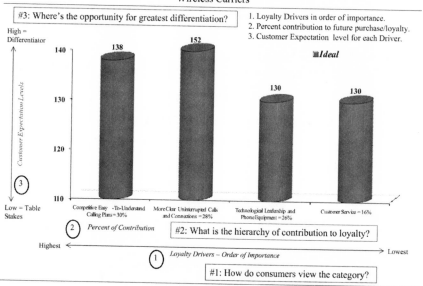

Despite the simple labels on the category drivers, each is made up of multiple attributes, benefits, and values. For each component, the individual percent-contribution to the driver in which it is located is also provided. That makes decision-making far easier and facilitates internal strategic alignment.

The height of the bars — expressed in indices — indicates the level of expectation that consumers hold for each of the drivers. Keep in mind that it is possible for a consumer to have a higher expectation level for a less important driver. Interestingly, this is usually seen in more rational drivers like *Price* where it is not — except in the case of commodities — the most important driver, but rather the driver for which consumers hold very high expectations. They want to pay as little as possible for whatever product or service they're considering.

The indices are benchmarked against 100, so a 115 means that the expectation for the driver is 15 percent higher than the norm. The higher the index, the higher the level of expectation a consumer holds for that particular driver.

Category Ideals and brands (and brand-variables, like media and sponsorship opportunities) can be examined on an overall basis via a single index number representing the weighted-average of the four drivers. A higher index is better than a lower index. Some things in research *never* change!

Real loyalty and engagement metrics are not static and unchanging. They are fluid and shift — as you will see in the upcoming Starbucks example. Shifts in values show up faster with engagement and loyalty metrics (usually 12 to 18 months) than they do via traditional research and marketing efforts. As they are predictive, they show up before changes on the brand balance sheet too.

Brands that best meet — or even exceed — the expectations consumers hold for the category drivers always attain higher levels of loyalty and thus, more positive consumer behavior in the marketplace. Marketing mismanagement notwithstanding, brands that are assessed better versus the Ideal are always more profitable than the competition. Always.

But to compound the difficulties, just when a brand manager or executive feels that he really understands what drives loyalty in their category, the drivers shift in importance — in some cases moderately, but in other cases, profoundly. Category drivers — and the category and customer attributes, benefits, and values they consist of — are critically important to understanding brand engagement, loyalty, and getting it right when dealing with today's 'bionic' consumers. Properly configured, category drivers will tell you far more than who a consumer is beyond the typical demographic and attitudinal factors.

In 2008, for the first time in 11 years, all but two of the 57 categories tracked in the annual Brand Keys *Customer Loyalty Engagement Index* have shown a shift in the drivers of consumer loyalty and engagement. That's 26,000 consumers, 18 to 65 years of age drawn from the nine US Census Regions, who self-selected the categories in which they are consumers, and the brands for whom they are customers. Eighty-five percent of the population was interviewed by phone and fifteen percent face-to face, to account for today's population who are cell phone-only consumers.

Keep in mind that the importance of the category loyalty drivers is identified from the loyalty metrics themselves. They reveal what people think and not what they *say* they think. These figures are not derived importance or stated importance. And do not make the mistake of thinking them comparable.

When you see numbers like these from that many people, you can't help but visualize the part of the movie where the scientists are drinking coffee in the lab and suddenly a machine that never beeps starts to beep because somewhere the floor of the ocean has cracked open. Shifts like these are a warning that marketers had better start listening for that beep because they tell you what you really need to know as a brand:

what consumers will actually be doing in the real marketplace.

That only matters, of course, if you're keeping score by counting your sales and profits and not merely satisfaction or awareness levels.

12. Reasonable people should be able to agree on a reasonable definition of "Brand Equity." "Engagement" too.

With a predictive leading-indicator Ideal established, you now have a yardstick you can use to drive strategy as well as the basis for comparison for why your brand may be chosen over and over again. Ultimately, it all depends on how the brand measures up to the Ideal and the customer and category values that shape it. Again, this has nothing to do with "awareness," "familiarity," or "imagery."

So, we define "brand equity" as the brand's strengths compared to the Ideal as defined by the consumer. How well does the brand meet — or even exceed — expectations for the drivers of the category in which it competes?

Thus, we are able to submit the following equation, which also identifies a working definition for "engagement."

$$\Uparrow \text{Brand Equity} \Rightarrow \text{Loyalty} = \text{Profitability}$$

Translation: an increase in Brand Equity yields increased levels of Loyalty, which generates positive behavior in the marketplace, resulting in profitability.

Therefore, "engagement" is defined as the consequence of any marketing or communication effort that results in an increased level of brand equity for the product or service — and therefore engenders loyalty, a leading-indicator of sales and profitability.

This has been our working definition for over six years, and was the definition we provided in 2006 to the MI4 Steering Committee, a consortium made up of representatives of the *Advertising Research Foundation* (ARF), the *Association of National Advertisers* (ANA), and the *American Association of Advertising Agencies* (AAAA), seeking to define the anatomy of engagement.

At the time, definitions offered up by major media and client companies who presented their engagement philosophy and practice to the MI4 Steering Committee ranged from "awareness" to "time spent," and from "visitors per month" to "positive attitudes resulting from the communication." Definitions included "relevance" and "the consumer connection." "Getting the right message in front of the right audience at the right time" was suggested, as was "the audience (remaining) at the commercial break." Our word-of-mouth brethren suggested, "buzz was an indicator, a form, and a result of engagement."

Of all the companies presenting to the MI4 committee, only Brand Keys advocated a direct relationship between engagement and positive consumer behavior and sales.

In fairness, Bob Barocci, the ARF President, offered up the only other definition that had anything to do with engagement and commerce: "Engagement is a prospect's interaction with a marketing communication in a way that can be proven to be predictive of sales effects." You can see how close our definitions are, ours, albeit, more process-expressed. It was our opinion that anything that did not mention something to do with positive consumer behavior in the marketplace or sales or profitability, was not talking about real *brand* "engagement," but rather the various methods that drew a consumer's attention to the brand.

While engaging the consumer using entertainment — whether you are talking about the platform, the program, or the advertising — is an important first step, it is often mistaken for the desired end-result. Cool platforms running hot programming with funny ads can get the brand attention — but that may be all it does, and that's why definitions that talk about engagement from a media and advertising perspective are so loosely tied to in-market performance, if at all. The best advertising in the world in terms of breakthrough and branding is all show and no substance if there is not a loyalty-based consumer-centric strategy behind the message.

The MI4 Committee came up with the following working definition of engagement: "Engagement is turning on a prospect to a brand idea enhanced by the surrounding context." The shaky phrase in that description was, of course, "turning on," which meant different things to different people, depending upon which sector of the marketing, advertising, media, promotion, buzz, sponsorship, design, research, or production portion of the business one was talking about — or wanted to talk about.

Happily, in mid-2008, the newly established ARF Engagement Council produced a more behaviorally-explicit definition for the membership. It goes like this: "Generating relevant behavior with the customer or prospect," which could be applied to virtually any sector of the marketing and communications world, but finally injects behavior into the operative definition.

Real engagement should not only include strategy decisions, but advertising executions, communication efforts, promotions, sponsorships, co-branding, and media planning activities. Virtually anything that can be shown or told to the consumer about the brand, and its planned activities, can be measured for the level of engagement it *will* produce — predictively and in advance of spend, with absolute certainty.

Pre and post measures, much like Price-Earnings ratios, can be used to demonstrate *Brand Equity ROI,* quantifying the impact of any advertising, media, or marketing initiative.

13. *Media planning can be optimized. Integrated media can be measured.*

The need for a real measure for integrated media planning has been amplified in two ways. First, by the rapidly evolving ways in which consumers use, juggle, adopt, and "gate keep" old and new media. And second, in the way burgeoning "new" media technologies have become more and more regarded and relied upon as legitimate media platforms. Planning complexity cannot be denied and so it is critical that marketers measure their brand's interaction in this "ecology" — beyond demographics, reach and frequency, and CPMs.

Yes, some media formats are more practicable than others while others are more "cost-effective." Each touch point argues that they incorporate a unique set and subset of values, nuances, and capabilities to communicate, inform, and persuade that make them better than others. But ultimately, they cannot all be "above average," and the decision process has relied predominantly on traditional media measures — not real engagement assessments. Based upon the Brand Keys predictive

Brand-to-Media Engagement (B2ME) metrics — some media and platforms *are* actually more efficacious for certain categories and brands. But that too can be measured before the spend.

Today, marketers presenting in public forums literally throw their hands up and state, "Integrated media effects cannot be measured." This is patently untrue. Integrated engagement assessments can demonstrate the effects cross-media consumption has on a brand's equity and therefore, engagement levels — both positive *and* negative — as well as consumer behavior in the marketplace. Again, before the spend.

Currently, we examine 30+ media touch point platforms that *might* conceivably be consumed/seen/viewed/read/experienced individually and in combination with one another. And each comes with a validity study.

The model also acknowledges that relying upon cross-media consumption on a "time spent" interaction basis produces limited insights in terms of cross-media-generated consequences. This is equally true about relying on some assessment based on identifying media touch points that consumers "love," "trust," find "educational," or even think "inspiring." What's more, inferences made on the basis of percent of the media budget allocated to various touch points provide absolutely no insights or direction regarding an understanding of integrated communication effects. An engagement approach "equalizes" these media platforms on those bases, and the combined output allows marketers to better understand media consumption (as opposed to allocation).

Through the diagnostics, marketers can not only identify the impact media has on the success of a brand when used together, but also how — and in what ways — the media combinations work from a strategic brand management perspective. Media can then be allocated on a more synergistic and efficient basis which, in a more complex marketplace, is more critical to the success of a brand.

On the flip side, media venues and platforms (and promotion and sponsorship opportunities) can use loyalty-based engagement assessments to prove real aspects of differentiation and superiority — beyond audience access, visibility, and awareness opportunities.

14. *Brand differentiation is tougher, which is why engagement is so much more important.*

In our 2008 *Customer Loyalty Engagement Index,* there were more 'ties' in terms of brand loyalty rankings than ever before, even as category drivers were shifting as never before. The best you can say is that it is a sign of category standardization, but more likely that the curtain has been pulled back from brands, exposing products and services that have lost their 'brandness' and their meaning.

Our colleague and positioning expert Jack Trout kept it short and to the point: "differentiate or die." Companies that differentiate based upon loyalty insights and consumer expectations end up driving less-informed, undifferentiated competition out of business. Toyota and its dominance over GM springs to mind. Think of it as possessing more brand equity than the competition. Having the consumer believe that the brand can better meet or exceed what they hunger for (whether you are a quick-serve restaurant, a computer, or a media entity) is the ultimate solution.

But not everything is a brand — no matter what their levels of awareness and no matter how long they've been competing in the marketplace. Real brands have some resonating sense of meaning for the consumer, usually emotional, and are always difficult to measure via traditional image-based approaches.

In 2005, we conducted a study in the US and the UK examining nearly 1,700 products and services. The test was conducted to determine to what degree these products and services were a) imbued with some degree of meaning (at that point we'd accept either emotional *or* rational meaning) and b) were significantly differentiated from the competition.

We expected that we'd end up with a scale that began with "commodities" on one end and "human brands" on the other. And in the middle would reside "brands."

That's what we expected.

It turned out that there were plenty of products and services that had universally high levels of awareness and virtually no resonating values, emotional or otherwise. They were known, but they weren't known for anything in particular. Everyone knew their names, but not why they were different from one another or why one should matter to them more than another.

They had become well-known, but totally undifferentiated products or services — "Category Placeholders." Everyone knew them, but nobody knew them for anything in particular. Like GM, who has become the ACME Car Company of the 21st century. The final continuum looked something like this:

Figure 1.2
Brand Keys Commodity-to-Human Brand Continuum (U.S.)

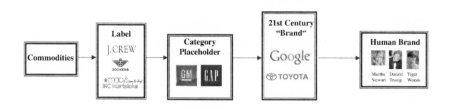

Don't misunderstand us. Real product or service differentiation *is attainable* if you have something new and different that better meets or exceeds customer expectations. You just need to know what those expectations are and where you'll get the greatest return from your efforts and investment. And it turns out that emotional differentiation is always more leverageable and successful and ownable than rational differentiation. There were always MP3 players available, but look what happened to the marketplace when Apple introduced the iPod. Sanyo was the first phone manufacturer to add a camera to their cell phones — an act more out of product differentiation desperation than anything else. Forty-three days later Samsung introduced their camera phone. Now try finding a cell phone without a camera. Virtually impossible. Name another iPod-like competitor-brand. Also virtually impossible.

15. Celebrities are not brands.

Supermodels are not brands. Neither are athletes or musicians. If the first thing you think of is the last action movie an actor starred in, or how many gold medals an athlete has won or gold albums a musician has earned, or the last *Sports Illustrated* swimsuit spread or Victoria's Secret catalog in which they were featured, that doesn't make them brands. That makes them celebrities.

And it doesn't guarantee "engagement." Attention? Absolutely. Hero-worship, perhaps. Admiration? Lust and/or desire? Almost certainly. But it doesn't make them brands. It makes them celebrities, athletes, musicians, and supermodels with new income streams. It makes them spokespeople or endorsers, but not brands.

In some small way it can provide heightened visibility for a new perfume offering, for example, or in a slightly larger way, some short-term differentiation, and in a larger way, a personal endorsement. It certainly makes whatever product or service they're shilling for something more than a commodity. But just standing next to, wearing, or putting their name on a product doesn't make them a brand. Because beyond their fame, athletic prowess, musical talent, or beauty, you'd be hard pressed to articulate any meaningful value they, or their commercial offering, personify. Try coming up with three positive and leverageable values for Paris Hilton, the world's most inexplicably famous woman. Or something for Michael Phelps that doesn't have to do with swimming or water. See what we mean? So don't call them brands. It only encourages them!

16. If you want to measure real engagement, loyalty metrics can be applied to any aspect of brand and marketing.

Just that. Any aspect, any category — B2B or B2C — in branding or marketing or communications or media planning can be viewed through a consumer loyalty and engagement lens. The following chapters demonstrate that, and provide a real-world example and a validity study for each.

17. There are critical questions you need to be able to comfortably and intelligently answer if you want to profitably engage customers.

Any brand that can correctly answer all of these questions has a firm grasp on its loyalty metrics and engagement outcomes — and will have profits you can bet on. To how many of the following questions does your brand have predictive, correlated-to-behavior and profitability answers?

- Do you have predictive loyalty and engagement metrics in place? (Operative word is "predictive." Everybody *claims* to have loyalty measures!)

- What are the leading-indicator drivers of loyalty and engagement for your category?

- What individual attributes, benefits, values, imagaic items, and communication elements make up the drivers? (You may be calling them image, essence, or personality items. Some companies even refer to them as "brand DNA." Nomenclature doesn't matter. Can you identify them and the percent-contribution they each make to loyalty and engagement?)

- What is the order of importance of the drivers in your category?

- How do they change, consumer segment to consumer segment?

- What percent-contribution does each driver make to loyalty, engagement, and profitability?

- What expectations do consumers hold for each of the drivers in your category? (And does that also change consumer segment to consumer segment?)

- How does this vary by product or service offering? By region or country?

- On which drivers is your brand strong or weak?

- How does your brand perform versus the competition?

- What's your brand equity? How well does your brand meet or exceed the expectations consumers hold for the category?

- What are consumers willing to believe about your brand? (A word of warning: saying it, doing it, and doing it believably are three entirely different things.)

- Which market opportunities can your brand actually sustain?

- Which above-and-below-the-line media will optimize engagement with your brand? (We're not asking about audience demographics. You — and your competitors — already know all there is to know about that area!)

- Can you quantify the impact of your marketing and advertising efforts, and do those metrics correlate to sales or fiscal return-on-investment?

- And, are these predictive and not after-the-fact, 20:20 hindsights?

- And, finally, are you absolutely certain?

18. *Loyalty and engagement metrics can be easily incorporated into any traditional research efforts.*

Because real loyalty and engagement assessments are predictive, making them part of your marketing and research toolbox can supercharge your traditional research efforts.

You can, for example, overlay loyalty assessments on your questionnaires to identify high percent-of-contribution areas of inquiry. Why ask questions that have little or no impact on how the consumer will behave toward your brand when you can insert loyalty metrics into your brand tracking and turn tracking into prediction?

You can use loyalty and engagement insights to segment focus group respondents on the basis of brand bonding levels or how they really view the category. Or, use the brand strengths and weaknesses or identification of drivers with high expectation levels as a way of optimizing your discussion guides.

You can also integrate loyalty and engagement metrics into your communication checks and determine how well your message is delivering against strategic loyalty drivers, and identify which creative option best reinforces brand values. You can even use loyalty and engagement assessments as a way of building a visual vocabulary for your brand. We'll show you how in Chapter 3.

19. *The brand should be the beneficiary of all your marketing investments.*

Marketing and advertising is not a leisure pursuit — it is a business. It's an investment in the brand and like all investments, companies and shareholders expect returns on their investments. You ought to be able to optimize your investment and have predictive assessments that allow you to do just that.

But Lord Leverholm's or John Wanamaker's observation that "half their advertising budget was being wasted — they just didn't know which half," while remarkably similar today, needs to be updated for the 21st century's more complex and expensive media ecology. It's likely that more than half of the budget is being wasted. Marketers just don't know.

What marketers do know is that the ad ran on TV or radio, or appeared in a magazine or newspaper, or on a website, or that their signage appeared at the stadium — and that's pretty much all they know. Most media options talk about audience size, demographics, show ratings, and crowd counts. But, that was supposed to be what they were providing in the first place. And they got paid for their time or space or signage or sponsorship opportunity.

But the brand needs something more that just the option of being seen. They're looking for some precise measure of what effect running their advertisement on a particular cable or broadcast network, or in one magazine versus another, had on the consumer. Was brand image improved *vis à vis* the category Ideal or the competitive set? Did sales ensue? What exactly did you get?

To provide these assessments we've adapted our customer loyalty metrics and created a Brand-to-Media Engagement model.

It is an engagement-based adjunct to traditional media planning and can chart the precise effects attributable to a brand's appearance in a particular media vehicle. Certain media properties and platforms can actually reduce attention levels and degrade brand equity while others can greatly enhance them. This is true no matter how appropriate the editorial environment, how popular the venue, or how large the appropriately-configured audience demographic. Audiences, viewers, readers, consumers, customers, and prospects should end up being engaged.

20. When it comes to your brand, you <u>can</u> always be right!

Marketers who possess a predictive solution, both innovative enough to deal with bionic consumers, and comprehensive enough to deal with virtually any marketing initiative on any media platform, are going to come away with insights and assessments that are, quite literally, prophetic.

When you can anticipate the needs, wants, and expectations of your various audience segments and have access to value propositions that really drive consumer behavior in the marketplace, you'll have 20:20 foresight. When you know how well your brand meets or exceeds consumer expectations and how well your communications perform against those expectations, you'll be able to calculate ROI assessments *before* you spend your money — and invest more wisely.

With real customer loyalty metrics, you receive *leading-indicators* of consumer purchase behavior, engagement, sales, and profitability. That lets your brand be deliberate — not reactive — in all your brand and marketing efforts.

Because, when you have real loyalty and engagement metrics, you'll be the smartest person in the procurement meeting. And that lets you turn the bet on your brand into a certainty.

THE KEYHOLE:

PEEKING AT 21ST CENTURY BRANDS:

January 30, 2006

LOYALTY PROCEEDS PROFITABILITY. ALWAYS!

Loyalty is a leading-indicator of profitability.

Let me put that another way: if you have loyal customers, you can virtually bet the farm that your company will be profitable!

Here's a shorthand version: Loyalty = $$$.

The reason I repeated all that is last Tuesday the automotive tracking firm, R. L. Polk, presented their 10th Annual 2006 Automotive Loyalty Awards. They announced that General Motors "outpaced the rest of the industry in manufacturer loyalty," winning for the 6th consecutive year in the "Overall Manufacturer" category.

Last Friday, however, *The New York Times* reported: "GM Posts Worst Loss Since 1992: Deficit for 2005 is $8.6 Billion." Eight billion! That's an eight with nine zeros following it! One of the reasons for this loss, noted the *Times* was "GM sold 150,000 fewer large SUVs in 2005 than in 2004." I guess they didn't see the Polk press release.

Anyway, Brand Keys measures loyalty too. We invented the metrics and we have an award too. It's called (take a deep breath) "The *Brandweek Customer Loyalty Awards. . .*powered by Brand Keys" and it's given out in April. Our measures *are* predictive. An independent corporate valuation firm found Brand Keys assessments correlated as high as .901 with company profitability. So it makes me wonder just how GM was able to "outpace the rest of the industry" and lose more money than the Gross National Products of some countries!?

If you're wondering too, the press release said that they got the award because 63% of GM owners returning to market in 2005 opted for another new GM vehicle. Maybe that was 63% of only 100 drivers. Or 1,000. However you do the math, it clearly wasn't enough to make GM profitable. That kind of math gives economics rigor, but alas, in this case, also mortis.

By our measures, the automotive brand engendering the highest loyalty is Toyota. They earned $11 billion in 2005, and expect to exceed that this year. Relying on research that tells you what people were thinking about yesterday and not what they're going to do tomorrow, is like driving a car using only a rearview mirror to steer. Not, you'll admit, the smartest way to manage your automotive brand, or any other brand for that matter! We prefer to be looking ahead through the windshield.

Anyway, loyalty = $$$. If you measure it right.

2 years and 7 months later. . .

General Motors announced its losses widened to $15.5 billion in the second quarter of 2008 as North American sales plummeted. The loss of $27.33 per share is the third-worst quarterly loss in the automaker's history.

2

How Starbucks Lost its Buzz

All my life, I always wanted to be somebody. Now I see that I should have been more specific.

Jane Wagner

There is no better contemporary story than that of Starbucks to demonstrate the imperative of understanding what matters to the consumer, what differentiates your brand, and what will drive loyalty, sales, and profits. Everybody's heard the story of how the original Starbucks (the name taken from Herman Melville's *Moby Dick*) opened in Pike Place Market in Seattle, Washington, in 1971. Its purpose: to sell great coffee beans. Howard Schultz joined the company in 1982, and after a trip to Milan, Italy, suggested that the company sell coffee *and* espresso drinks in addition to coffee beans. The original founders rejected this idea. They believed that offering up brewed coffee, lattes, and mochas would distract the company from its *raison d'être*. To them, coffee was something to be prepared and, generally speaking, consumed at home.

Certain that there was much money to be made selling recreational coffee beverages in an Americanized

European coffeehouse environment, Schultz started the *Il Giornale* coffee bar chain in 1985. Two years later the original owners sold the Starbucks chain to Schultz's *Il Giornale* company, who quickly re-branded their stores as Starbucks and began to expand. The rest, as they say, is branding history. Or will be.

It is reasonable to presume that few can be found who have not heard of the Starbucks brand. It solved the "awareness problem" twenty years ago as it began its march from Seattle to the streets of New York, where at last count 161 stores (or one store for every 57,852 people) puts one only minutes away when caffeine levels dip dangerously low. Much like other mega brands, such as Ford and Coke, a ubiquitous brand presence has remained stable while profits have not. Being aware of a brand, while a necessary condition, is highly insufficient when it comes to the ultimate evaluation of success: the balance sheet.

Unfortunately for Starbucks, awareness of the brand is all too keen these days, as the media reports on ill-considered breakfast sandwiches, promotions, store closings, declining stock prices, and its various attempts at couponing to boost sagging profits. With thousands of stores in 44 countries, Starbucks has by no means disappeared. It is, however, clearly a brand in danger of obsolescence — as hard as that might be for today's consumer to imagine. Then again, it was hard for the generation before to imagine a world without Pan American Airlines, Montgomery Ward Department Stores, and Kinney Shoes. But here we are.

So what happened to a brand that at one point in its history was rumored to be opening a store somewhere every day of the work-week? Is it simply a slowing economy that has caused the planned closure of 600 US Starbucks' stores this year? Or is there another reason, one that dominates the vagaries of the Dow Jones? If our careers in brand research have taught us nothing else, it is that price is as fluid a variable in customer loyalty as they come. If everyone wanted to pay the lowest price possible for his or her out-of-home coffee experience, the local gas station with the cloudy pour-it-yourself pot would suffice. It's value that consumers want, and expect. And in that, so said William, lies the rub.

In one of the most compelling brand stories of our time, the data leads the way to what went wrong, and continues to go wrong, with this impressive brand. There may still be time, but only if Starbucks looks at its brand from the customer side of the barista bar.

YOU ACTUALLY *CAN* GET THERE FROM HERE

For Starbucks, early 2006 was still a very good year. The clouds that would block the light of the logo had yet to appear. Four critical drivers governed Loyalty in the category. These are (alphabetically) *Location and Value, Quality and Taste, Service and Surroundings,* and *Variety and Selection.* In January 2006, our *Customer Loyalty Engagement Index* metrics in the Coffee Category demonstrated Starbuck's dominance over Dunkin' Donuts and McDonald's (who was in the process of developing what would turn out to be an extraordinarily successful premium coffee strategy and offering, but had yet to go national). This was especially true in the driver of customer loyalty and engagement called *Service and Surroundings* — a driver in the coffee category that the brand itself had shaped. They had, after all, imported a European coffeehouse-like experience; comfy chairs, free newspapers to read, an unhurried experience. At the outset you could literally close your eyes and feel as if you were sitting at Les Deux Magots on the Saint Germain des Pres in Paris, sans the disdainful waiters. Starbucks rose on the bar charts like a skyscraper in suburbia, dwarfing the competition.

Figure 2.1
2006 Customer Loyalty Engagement Index: Coffee

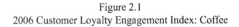
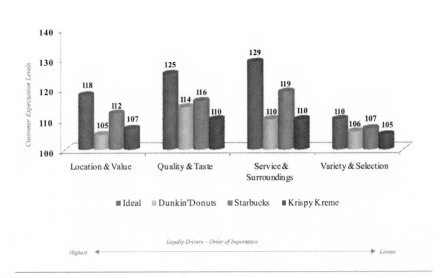

While all the brands fell short of the customer expectations for the Ideal coffee brand, Starbucks' customers were still, in the beginning of 2006, rating the brand better than the customers of the competitive brands on meeting those expectations. This was true for the driver of loyalty and engagement that had the highest expectations — *Service and Surroundings* — and offered the greatest potential for differentiation among the brands. But among category observers, this was not a surprise. Starbucks had, after all, literally re-defined the category in the United States.

Often, change seems to come upon us suddenly. But a loss of brand dominance is not usually an overnight phenomenon, only an awareness of it is. When things become obvious because they have already happened, there appears in the backward glance to have been many signs along the way —harbingers that were not attended to and shifts that were dismissed as irrelevant. This is of no consolation to a brand that has to pay the high costs of damage control, restructuring, and the sheer pain of turning it around. For us, the worst thing of all was to have watched the Starbucks story unfold when we had data demonstrating that they were losing their dominance to Dunkin' Donuts — *before* it happened in the marketplace.

At the end of 2006, our data demonstrated that the coffee category was going through a seismic shift in brand performance:

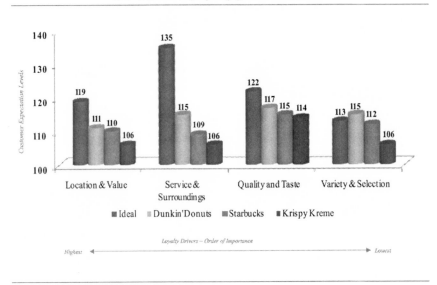

Figure 2.2
2007 Customer Loyalty Engagement Index: Coffee

Three things happened at the end of that year: the *Service and Surroundings* driver moved up in importance, from third to second; customer expectations for the driver also increased; and Starbucks, for the first time, lost its dominance by a significant margin to Dunkin' Donuts. It is only fair to note that Dunkin' had been making some extraordinary strides in their branding campaign during this period. "America Runs On Dunkin™" was getting a lot of notice. More importantly, its message was resonating with coffee drinkers. After checking the data yet one more time, there was only one conclusion: Starbucks' customers were expressing their disappointment with the brand in the area it was known for — that European coffee experience that had built the brand.

So, what happened?

We released our data in January of 2007 as part of the *Customer Loyalty and Engagement Index*, published annually by *Brandweek*. A drop in performance of a major brand often results in a flood of interview requests from reporters who want more detail for their business columns. But the silence was deafening.

The Euro-cool Starbucks losing to the blue-collar Dunkin' brand? The disbelief was palpable — understandable when the messenger is predicting rain as the (brand) sun is shining. Understandable, but nonetheless wrong. Starbucks' customers were no longer ceding dominance to the brand they claimed as their own. We knew that. The *Service and Surroundings* driver and the attributes, benefits, and values (ABVs) that comprise it made it clear that something had happened to the experience the Starbucks' customers had received in exchange for their loyalty and engagement with the brand. Having repeatedly seen the predictive nature of our metrics, we trusted that trouble was not far away. And we didn't have to wait long.

On February 14, 2007, *The Wall Street Journal* printed the text of an internal memo sent by Howard Schultz, CEO, entitled "The Commoditization of the Starbucks Experience." While never intended to be read outside of the company, much less published in one of the most widely read newspapers in the country, it had been leaked to the press. It quickly became known as "the Schultz memo" and the private concerns of a CEO voiced to his inner circle were soon fodder for public speculation.

In the memo, Schultz states that the growth, development, and scale of Starbucks over the previous ten years, going from less than 1,000 stores to 13,000, led to decisions that resulted in what he termed "the commoditization of our brand." He continued,

> Many of these decisions were probably right at the time, and on their own merit would not have created the dilution of the experience; but in this case, the sum is much greater and, unfortunately, much more damaging than the individual pieces. For example, when we went to automatic espresso machines, we solved a major problem in terms of speed of service and efficiency. At the same time, we overlooked the fact that we would remove much of the romance and theatre that was in play with the use of the La Marzocca machines.

Days later, the *New York Times* published an article called "Give me a Double Shot of Starbucks Nostalgia" that spoke to the memo originally intended for only Schultz's top executives:

> Last week, Mr. Schultz was on vivid display when an internal memo he wrote to his top executives was leaked to Starbucksgossip.com. . . He pointed, for instance, to the company's decision some years ago to install automatic

espresso machines, which, he wrote, "solved a major problem in terms of speed and service," but also made buying a cup of Starbucks coffee a more antiseptic experience.

Suddenly, our phone began to ring. Reporters were interested in the metrics out there that quantitatively predicted what Schultz had suspected and that were beginning to prove out in the marketplace. The *New York Times* included us in the story, and we shared what we knew — the European coffeehouse experience was no longer how people thought of the Starbucks brand. Success was a double-edged sword. Starbucks was popular – and crowded. So they got rid of the comfy chairs and free newspapers to make room for the lines of customers and not have them linger. Their process needed to work more quickly, so they didn't grind the beans anymore. And without the grinding of the beans, the stores didn't smell like coffee shops and they didn't sound like real coffee shops. Without hand-pulled shots, "the theatre," as Schultz himself noted, was gone. And with that, the sense that the beverage you were waiting on line for was definitely not being crafted especially for you. What was coming out of the urn might very well have been of high quality. It just didn't seem to be worth the money, particularly when a similar product was available just down the block and far less expensive. At Dunkin Donuts, for example.

As customer loyalty metrics are leading-indicators of consumer behavior and, ultimately, profitability, eight months later Starbucks' share price had fallen by 43 percent! This is yet another instance of how the weakening of emotional elements is felt in both the marketplace *and* the balance sheet. All the rational elements were firmly in place: everybody knew the brand, knew where to buy it, and was willing to pay a premium price for what was generally a consistent product offering. Until, that is, the added-value, the experience, was removed from the equation.

There was no glee for us in being right, then or now, as Starbucks' troubles continue. Our 2008 data tells that story exceedingly well:

Figure 2.3
2008 Customer Loyalty Engagement Index: Coffee

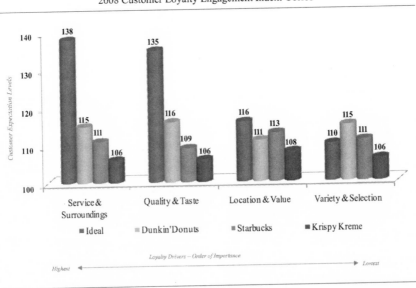

Again, as loyalty metrics are predictive of how consumers will behave toward a brand, customers stayed away in droves, making Starbucks' executives jittery and profits watery. Part of the reason for this had to do with the fact that in some coffee-deprived state-of-mind, Starbucks spent three years walking away from a successful brand position and a differentiating recreational coffee experience, and toward a doorway labeled "LIFESTYLE BRAND."

Starbucks has taken some measures — unfortunately absent from these predictive consumer engagement metrics. Mistaking *Variety and Selection* for *Service and Surroundings* — and a marketing foray for a brand strategy — they introduced a new blend. And when that didn't work they turned to some of the more traditional promotional devices to try to perk up sales, but stopped short of offering up a dollar menu because, according to Starbucks spokesmen, they didn't want to clash with Starbucks' luxury image. Yes, nothing says "luxury" like "a $1 discount on a cold drink after 1 PM" — a recent attempt the Starbuck's brand obviously felt they were reduced to offering.

In late June 2008, Starbucks announced that it will close 600 stores and will eliminate as many as 12,000 jobs. Why? Because customer traffic is down and Starbucks didn't focus on what actually drove loyalty.

We wish that were the moral of the story, but there's more. We are talking about the interaction of consumers and categories and not a mastodon frozen in ice; neither categories nor consumers are static or constant. Not only did the drivers of loyalty shift, but the consumer set changed as well. Not only did Starbucks help to create the new category, but they were directly responsible for educating the consumers about the category.

Suddenly, customers whose experience with out-of-home coffee that had been limited to ordering "black" or "regular," *i.e.* coffee with sugar and milk, were now "experts" about coffee beverage formats, ordering all sorts of exotic combinations and permutations. Not only did the consumers change, but the category morphed as well. The local coffee shop with the black and regular offering all of a sudden saw a market opportunity. "If folks want this latte stuff," they reasoned, "why not give it to them?" So they did. And the competitive set grew. Quality of offering improved, and pretty soon there wasn't a major city anywhere where you couldn't get a more-than-acceptable, economical, non-Starbucks, mocha latte. What had once been "delight" was now "expectation," which is why a generation of consumers won't think twice about getting their recreational coffee beverages from McDonald's!

The Starbucks story, and the coffee category itself, illustrates why we refer to this data as consumer-generated metrics. As researchers, we do not create the drivers. We do not put them in a hierarchy of importance, nor do we attach the level of expectation. Consumers do that. While we use our Jungian-based instrument and process of analyses to get to that data, we don't create it. It is the consumer who benchmarks the categories in those three critical dimensions of importance, hierarchy, and expectations. In an industry where the word "consumer" is put in front of nearly everything, we can use that term with supreme confidence.

It is precisely because our metrics for the coffee category are consumer generated, that it predicted in-market performance for the Starbucks brand. Customers began to question what made Starbucks worth the price now that the customized feeling of handcrafted beverages, along with the comfy couches of the "third place," were gone. Dunkin' was ready with exactly the right value strategy and down-home message. Sure, a slowing economy didn't help, but it wasn't the economy that broke the brand's winning streak. Starbucks was *not* understanding what the customer *really wanted* from the brand, and how important the coffee-consumption experience really was. If that was gone, why not grab a medium latte in the pink and white cup and pay a lot less for it? And soon, Starbucks had solved the problem. The lines were shorter, but not because they were moving customers through. There were not as many customers.

SO, WHERE TO?

As Schultz pointed out in his memo, the challenges to Starbucks then were very real. The obstacles today are no less challenging. But the data offers authentic signposts to brand gold. Certainly, *Variety and Selection*, a driver where Starbucks, with its 87,000+ beverage possibilities actually *exceeds* the Ideal, is not the place to dig. This driver is lowest in importance and table-stakes to the customer. Offering a new "Pike Place

Roast®" — yet another selection — may get some press, but will certainly not save the brand. Nor will dollar cups of coffee. Customers didn't trade brands because of price; they became unwilling to pay the price when the experience had disappeared.

There is far more nuance and granularity in the data than is prudent to go into here. Each driver contains the attributes, benefits, and values that consumers link together, along with the percent-contribution those items make to loyalty. Our experience with brands is that small details can sometimes be a marker to the kind of bold strategic moves that turn treading water into sailing. And while there is currently no widely adopted standard of grading coffee, there is a standard for grading the coffee consumption experience — loyalty metrics that tell you what the customer really wants.

By understanding what the customer really wants, anything is possible for the brand that delivers it. We wish Starbucks the best and encourage the brand to get more specific about who they really are — an identity built on what they once did even better than making drinks: creating loyal customers.

THE KEYHOLE:
PEEKING AT 21ST CENTURY BRANDS:

September 13, 2007

WAKE UP AND SMELL THE PROFITS

We track the Coffee category in our *Customer Loyalty Engagement Index.* Respondents self-select categories and brands for which they are, in fact, customers, and those are the brands they rate.

But brands themselves only get listed if enough respondents describe themselves as "customers." So we haven't been surprised to find that, for the past few years, McDonald's hasn't been showing up on our final list (They *do* show up in the Fast Food Restaurant category). They sold, of course, a lot of coffee, but in the past it wasn't "premium" in the way customers have come to expect, and it wasn't consumed enough on a regular AM basis. But McDonald's got smart and went premium and, at last count, had added coffee drinks (costing on average 26% less than those at Starbucks) at two-thirds of its nearly 14,000 stores over the past year. And, in a *Consumer Reports* taste test, they beat out all comers.

So in looking at some of the Wave Two *Customer Loyalty Engagement Index* data we weren't surprised to find the following rankings:

1. Dunkin' Donuts
2. McDonald's
3. Starbucks
4. Krispy Kreme

As usual, the loyalty and engagement metrics correlate nicely with sales, and profitability, with McDonald's posting August same-store sales of +8.1%, with analysts predicting that McDonald's shares will rise 18% in the coming year. Shares of Starbucks are down 24% this year, and they're down from #1 in 2006.

So we think that it's fair to say that from a loyalty perspective the only thing more stimulating than a good cup of coffee are increasing same-store sales and bigger profits.

9 months and 10 days later. . .
Fast Food News reported ". . . if Starbucks' answer is to retreat to the high end where margins are bigger and to try to defend that turf (against McDonald's) they will find themselves rapidly marginalized into a smaller and smaller niche as the low-end catches up and takes a large chunk of their market."

3

And Now for a Word from Your Customer:
The Over-Messaged and Under-Sold Consumer

The trouble with America isn't that the poetry of life has turned to prose, but that it has turned to advertising copy.

Louis Kronenberger

It's hard to believe with all the creative muscle flexed against the making of advertising that it doesn't do a better job for the brands that commission it. Contrary to the "hidden persuader" perception of brand as "brainwasher," the majority of brand advertising fails to motivate consumers to take the desired action that is the primary reason for the exercise in the first place. Any researcher who has banged his or her head against a 4-inch thick tracking study deck wondering why, after all the spend, nothing more than a blip has registered for the brand has surely been tempted to say, "advertising doesn't work," period. That's not the case, of course — but with such poor in-market "results" it's certainly tempting to declare a moratorium on traditional advertising and spend the money putting bumper stickers on flying monkeys instead.

To begin with, it should be acknowledged that it is hard not to be cynical with a business as difficult as advertising. Advertising to consumers is like talking to a teenager — they are, to say the least, inattentive and usually far more interested in their own lives than the message emanating from the parental, or television, unit. That is why, understandably so, the creators of advertising have tried all sorts of things to get the consumer's attention. It is no accident that as media and messaging has proliferated, so has the percentage of humorous ads. Entertainment is a very big part of breakthrough, and is in no danger of being ignored by advertising agencies trying to get the brand "seen" in a more and more cluttered media ecology. Some very creative executions have certainly been developed, especially as computer-generated graphics have entered the fray. Yet, one wonders if these campaigns get more press than profits. Slick ads for the Gap, for example, while artistic and pretty, have so far failed to do nearly their return-on-investment (ROI) part to reverse the decline of same store sales. And the Super Bowl is an annual reminder of ads-as-show, but often with little substance when it comes to engagement with the brand.

Advertising *is* a tough business but not for the obvious reason of breakthrough, however. That is a challenge, most certainly, but not insurmountable — especially with the level of talent funneled out of unprofitable careers in the arts and into the agency business.

No, advertising is a tough business because it's a *strategic business.* Good, effective strategies that might reinforce brand equity and differentiate brands are more and more difficult to come by. More often than not, brands approach advertising as if it's a magic kingdom that exists outside of brand strategy, free of the rules of the business road because it's "storytelling" or "movie-making" or some other creative-sounding phrase that causes normally hands-on business people who usually ask tough questions to nod at the creatives like bobble head dolls. It's only later, after the advertising has made the list of the top-recalled ads of the week in one of the industry trades but has done little to boost sales, that whispers are heard at Home Office about how "they never even understood what the ad was really about," or something along those lines.

As the recent Jerry Seinfeld/Microsoft pairing proved, having money to spend is no guarantee that it will be spent wisely. Overwhelmingly, the initial offering of the $300 million Microsoft campaign, designed to fire back at Apple's brilliant "Mac versus PC" ads, has been declared across the blogosphere and media as a disaster. The consistent thread in the comments? No one seemed to understand what the ads were actually trying to say. Pulled after a mere two weeks on air, Microsoft's claim that they were always intended as a "teaser," and not destined for a longer run, is hard to buy — as is any reason for buying a PC over a Mac.

The Microsoft ads are not funny. But, even if they were, the standard they are being held to is that of Apple's amazing advertising about the PC and Vista — ads so funny they bear up under repeated viewing — and how those ads *sell* the Mac with not only a brand position but the proof points to back it up, something increasingly out of vogue in these days of ad-as-slapstick. One is left wondering what exactly the Microsoft campaign was intended to do. If not built for the heavy lifting of actually creating an in-market result, was it at least supposed to muscle us into a new way of feeling about Microsoft? If so, what new information were we supposed to take away from this ad? That in the PC-Apple wars, Microsoft is the nerd who, no matter how many zabillion dollars it has, still can't figure out how to dress itself?

The PC as un-cool. Got it. But we already knew that. You know who told us? Apple.

According to Microsoft, the campaign was a success, designed to "...create conversation and reintroduce Microsoft to the consumer dialogue." Again, a job Apple was doing amazingly well, as were the rants about Vista's inadequacies heard 'round the world. It is the worst defense of any brand advertising, nonetheless advertising that came with a luxury-goods price tag, to say it was meant to make people *talk*. What the brand adds to the conversation is the problem advertising was created to solve. Like starlets who don't care what they're in the paper for as long as they are in the paper, brands drunk on celebrity and buzz owe an explanation to their shareholders, who are waiting up with the light on.

Recently, another campaign from Microsoft hit the airways, this one a far better return on Apple's serve. Using Apple's own caricature of PC to open the spot, the message is clear: Apple is trying to turn you, PC user, into a stereotype. A montage of diverse people, places and politics visually refute Apple's "cool kid" position — the right tact to take for a brand with massive market penetration. It reframes the argument, most notably away from any discussion of Microsoft Vista's challenges, which, when you don't have an answer, buys you some time. Microsoft will eventually have to respond to Apple's hard-hitting critique of Vista, but this campaign at least is in the business of positioning the brand and selling to its strengths. Viewing this ad makes it even more obvious, however, that the Seinfeld ads cannot be classified as a "teaser" for this new campaign — those first ads central premise being Microsoft "PC as clueless geek" stereotype.

It's tempting to think of advertising as requiring a trade-off, that it is impossible to both bring attention to a message and to sell something. But it's not impossible. It's just hard. It's done all the time by brands such as Allstate, Target, and Apple. Allstate's storytelling approach featuring Dennis Haysbert uses high-drama to grab the viewer, and then offers compelling and clear support statements for its Good Driver Rewards® product. Target, with its chic use of shape and color, stops the viewer who sits mesmerized by a montage of product displayed so artfully that the difference between WalMart and Target is painfully obvious. And, as noted above, Apple, with its brilliant use of humor as it faces off with the PC is not too busy being funny enough to get on YouTube (which it is) to state its unique selling proposition, repeatedly. Advertising has to do something much more difficult than entertain. Movies entertain. Films can do all sorts of things that ads can't. Not that they are always obeyed, but here's just a short list of some differences:

- Negative emotion in film can be unresolved — it does not have to create positive brand associations.

- Ads want you to do something; movies don't ask you to do anything but watch.

- Ads embrace reality; films suspend it.

- Ads are set up as some representation of the truth; movies are acknowledged as fantasy.

- You can't kill anyone in an ad. Ever.

While the producers of advertising have certainly blurred the line between a pure entertainment medium like movies and that of ads, there are valid reasons for their differences — and those reasons are because of the job advertising is hired to do for the brand. That's where the difficulty of the job comes in, because it is *not* simply entertainment. Its *raison d'être* is to sell something. To get consumers to get up and do something. To behave in a certain way. That's why ads shouldn't just sit there and make you laugh — though so many do. That's why they can't blatantly employ the violence and pornography that is the lifeblood of films. Because nobody wants their brand associated with those kinds of values — though some recent advertising has certainly smudged the line. Go Daddy is one example with its buxom spokesperson who was remembered after the Super Bowl for two things, and neither was brand related. And that's why ads have to offer some semblance of presenting the viewer with the truth — because the brand is asking you to believe something and do something. Ads can use entertainment to get attention, but they must not stop there. They must complete the job and deliver a relevant and *strategically sound proposition* to the consumer. And that's where the trouble begins.

Why trouble? Because so many brands are not in possession of a consumer-generated view of their category upon which to build a strategy. Thus, in making their advertising, they end up in the entertainment business and not in the brand business.

Having been in countless meetings on advertising, the arguments for breakthrough are quite familiar. A brand team will argue vehemently for advertising that gets attention, believing it will automatically increase engagement for the brand in the marketplace. That is not necessarily true, of course. Surely we can all recall talking with our friends about a "good" ad seen on television last night while being completely unable to recall the brand name in the telling the next day. Beer ads often fall into this category. The jokes are worth repeating but what they had to do with the brand is anyone's guess. The most you can say about them is that they create a "funny" persona for the brand, and maybe that type of humor speaks to a desirable demographic. Show me a beer ad that doesn't do that.

Attention is not awareness. Attention is execution-related, awareness is brand-related. Attention to advertising can lead to brand awareness among consumers certainly — but even that is highly insufficient if the ad lacks relevancy to the consumer that results in sales. Delirious over strong attention scores based on entertainment values, brands rationalize soft motivation-to-purchase measures by making the argument that engagement with an ad is analogous to engagement with the brand. That could not be further from the truth, as tempting as it might be to believe.

Human beings love to be entertained. Frankly, our love affair is not with the automobile, it's with entertainment. Witness all the ways that humans watch each other: whether on television, the Internet, or the iPod. We love shows of all kinds and are attracted to them, and commercials are no exception. Yet, that attraction is so often just that, and nothing more.

The list is endless of brands people know but have no loyalty to whatsoever. Colas, or bottled waters. Credit cards and overnight parcel delivery services. Maybe consumers even choose them, if they are on sale or it's convenient. Yes, yes, they know the brand but they don't know it for anything in particular except that at that moment it's cheap or convenient. So, yes, awareness of a brand is better than no awareness. But it's one scary place to rest, and certainly no substitute for brand engagement and loyalty. And no ad, no matter how entertaining, is pulling its media weight if it isn't strategic.

Strategy should never stop at the borders of the brand, yet more often than not it does. As such, brands end up creating advertising that is like a bad dinner date, talking all about themselves right through dessert while the consumer tunes out and wonders if they can still make it home in time for *Dancing with the Stars*. The problem with advertising, that it is all image and very little strategic substance, is most often a problem of relevance. And relevance cannot be created without knowing, for certain, what actually matters to the consumer.

When strategy is aligned with consumer-generated insights about the category — with what engages and drives loyalty — creating effective advertising becomes so much easier. A coherent consumer-based strategy allows the intellectual and creative energy of the ad team to be harnessed with clear direction and defined boundaries. Entertainment can stop the consumer and the brand can make it worth his time, instead of simply cracking jokes and titillating. Every creative worth their salary wants to be pointed in a direction, and to respond creatively to that direction. Disciplined creativity is what advertising is all about, and the successful agencies know that.

The consumer is the beginning of the ad-creation process, not the end. And while many brands believe they are doing their share of consumer research and boldly representing the Voice of the Consumer, more often than not it is traditional research that fails to get at what consumers really think.

Even ethnographic studies that observe how people shop, or how they interact with a brand, back into the consumer experience through the brand *instead of starting with how the consumer experiences the brand altogether.* Consumers don't shop brands, even when they look for them and buy them; consumers shop categories and use brands to articulate their needs and expectations.

Think of the amazing success of the iPod.

Prior to it coming on the scene, the consumer had myriad perfectly serviceable MP3 players to choose from, including entries from the major brands. Any customer satisfaction survey would likely have produced high marks for the established brands out there competing in the category — brands that now eat crumbs at the iPod's table. It is important to remember that Apple did not invent the MP3 player. It didn't need to. What Apple did was start with the consumer experience of the category, hand-held music devices, and revolutionized it by giving consumers what was *most relevant to them*: easy access to the music they wanted in the sexiest package on the planet. Consumers didn't care a bit about the brands. They cared about what the brands were delivering, as did the now-famous silhouette advertising that showed human beings moving to a customized soundtrack for their lives. And all over America MP3 players that were working just fine but were not iPods showed up in thrift stores, on eBay, or were thrown in the bottom of desk drawers.

Most brands fail to deeply appreciate the profound disinterest consumers have in them. Consumers engage with brands — yes, absolutely. But only through a category lens. That may be hard for brands to accept, but it is the truth nonetheless, and that's why shifts in category loyalty drivers are leading-indicators of upcoming changes in consumer and category values. Because, with absolute certainty, these drivers describe how consumers view, compare, and engage with brands in the category.

Advertising — no matter what platform it runs on, no matter what program it's embedded in, no matter what celebrity stars in it — cannot be considered successful unless it performs against strategy and not simply against an average. No matter how specific the benchmark claims to be. By holding advertising accountable to consumer-generated metrics of what matters in a category and what consumers expect, a brand can finally answer the question "is this a good ad?"

Creative testing, therefore, is not enough. Copy testing is, by its very nature, execution-focused. It studies the breakthrough power of an ad, the short-term saliency of the brand, self-reported measures of purchase intent, and the literacy test of whether they "got it." But clearly, getting the message and being engaged by it are often two mutually exclusive things. And, while brand ratings are a part of any copy-testing system and can be tracked, they tell you nothing about the hierarchy of importance of those ratings. You may come away knowing that an ad got an "above average" rating on one item and a "below average" rating on another, but how do you know if that's a good thing? What if the consumer is shopping the category and evaluating your brand against your competitors all the while feeling the value where you are turning in a sub-par performance is far more important than the value where you excel? What if something else altogether is where the consumer holds the highest expectations for the category and where the brand is most likely to differentiate itself and create loyalty? Are you, as a brand, okay not knowing that? Are you all right with *not* evaluating your advertising against that?

A vital addition to any creative research is strategic communications research. And, that research absolutely must get below the radar to the emotional information that a brand needs to maximize communications and use as its benchmark. In addition, in an increasingly-visual world, images used by brands must be understood for how they are "read" by the consumer, along with other category information. By connecting advertising visuals to category drivers, consumers help us help brands understand the visual vocabulary they are using. Over time, a visual dictionary of a category emerges — a database of resonant metaphors a brand can harness as it creates new communications.

It has been said that wars are won less on the battlefield than they are in the General's mind. The chaos of battle is not unlike the marketplace — thus, the proliferation of those sorts of metaphors. But it is apt here because war, like the marketplace, is chaotic. The best hope any side has is a clear strategic vision that allows those in charge of tactics to adapt and to create, all the while focusing on the objective handed out clearly by the brand. Too often, advertising agencies bear the brunt of blame for the utter absence of a consumer-centric strategy on the part of the brand. Left to create in a vacuum, is it any wonder that entertainment becomes the one card they can play and keep the account?

The best research offers a look ahead, not a backward glance. The brand-promiscuous consumer with more choices and power than ever is here to stay. Advertising that speaks to what he or she is not getting from his or her current brand — but wants — has the greatest chance of success. That means possessing predictive and strategic engagement metrics against which to create the advertising in the first place. Then one can evaluate its success. Because only then will the consumer not just be messaged but be sold.

THE KEYHOLE:
PEEKING AT 21ST CENTURY BRANDS:

January 25, 2007

CREATIVE NIGHTMARE

By now you've likely seen the ads for Rozerem, the newish insomnia drug. Those are the ones with Abe Lincoln and the beaver or groundhog or some sort of rodent in them. If you're thinking, "Oh, them. Yeah I see them everyplace, but I didn't understand what they were advertising," you weren't alone. Nearly everyone we've talked to about the campaign said that very same thing.

To be charitable, one might suggest that all the ads and creative media buys were merely teasers. Get the campaign noticed. Have people actually ask themselves, "What is this about?" Maybe pay more attention to the campaign just to figure it out. On the other hand, as the campaign trundles on, this is beginning to look more and more like a case for creativity for creativity's sake.

These days, brands and ad agencies are so desperate to "engage consumers" that some have forgotten that the business heir in is one that deals with "disciplined creativity." You know, creative that communicates the brand strategy in a way that gets consumers to behave positively towards you. Perhaps someone should have pointed out to the brand that, in the marketplace, it isn't creative unless it moves product. Getting noticed, talked about, even winning creative awards is no substitute for real engagement. Real engagement always correlates with positive consumer behavior and, ultimately, profitability.

How did this campaign do? It's been reported that between January and September 2006 Rozerem spent nearly $100 million on ads, but only earned $48.7 million in wholesale revenue. You do the math.

Many a small pill has been made large by the right kind of advertising, but it's those kinds of ROI numbers that keep marketers up at night!

1 year, 1 month, and 1 week later. . .
CNN Money reported that Rozerem's campaign featuring President Lincoln and a talking beaver as dream characters was one of the worst ad campaigns in the category. While amusing, it did not convey a message of restful sleep and, as a result, "hasn't done well while spending an awful lot of money."

4

The Magical Media Tour:
Turning Targets into Customers

*You're always infinitely far from any solution until the
minute you find it.*

Stephen Hawking

The best thing about innovation is that it's new. A true
innovation looks at a problem from another direction and
offers a solution that has not been previously available.
The worst thing about innovation? It's new. New can
mean untried and when brand survival hangs in the
balance, unacceptable risk.

The best innovative solutions are those that can
combine a new approach to a problem with a tested
— and market-proven — process. This is the kind of
innovation found in our approach to engagement-based
media planning. By employing the highly-validated
methodology we use for brand metrics in the study of
new media complexities, marketers can assess levels of
engagement attained via media selection and media mix.
By selecting media options for brands on the basis of the
media's abilities to better "engage" the target, marketers

can better connect — and more effectively communicate — with them.

The predictive Brand-to-Media Engagement (B2ME) model allows marketers and planners to accurately measure the levels of engagement that *will* result from advertising and communication efforts. The following case study answers the question: which particular cable channel is first among equals? This approach not only answers that question based on engagement, but in doing so permits more strategic and effective planning and execution that will help turn traditional "targets" into actual paying "customers." Most importantly, as these assessments are predictive, they can be conducted *before* marketers spend their money!

THE CHALLENGE

In the 21st century marketplace, *locating* marketing targets is easier than ever before. Our ability to manage the information in databases to create highly-specific and sometimes unreachable segments is almost mindnumbing. And the list of acceptable media options — some call them "consumer touch points" — gets longer every day. *Engaging* consumers, however, is more complex. And because of just how much media exists — so much, in fact, that it is now referred to as an ecology unto itself — increased options and increased levels of personal and electronic "gatekeeping" have turned it into the 21st century's marketing version of the Holy Grail.

Without actual "engagement," advertising and marketing efforts are just that; creative and communicative attempts aimed at what brands have identified as being appropriate audiences. And while marketers and planners can virtually guarantee target audiences will have the opportunity to be exposed to their messages, they cannot, unfortunately, guarantee that any positive outcome for the advertised brand will result from the marketing exercise—not with the traditional tools currently used.

This case study demonstrates a major step forward for media purveyors — both traditional and new — on how to provide increased levels of engagement for a brand.

A MEDIA ENGAGEMENT SURE THING 2.0

All marketers agree that the consumption and mix of media used to communicate advertising messages has a direct and consequential behavioral effect on the level of engagement attained by the advertised brand. Marketers have known this, in their gut, long before there were metrics to prove it. What marketers have struggled with, however, is getting beyond "eyeballs" and demographic measurements to create a truly strategic media plan — one built around the right media in the right combination. That was the solution we went after, and this case study featuring the Target retail brand demonstrates exactly how that can be accomplished before actually running advertising.

THE ENGAGEMENT RESEARCH

Rainbow Media Holdings LLC, a subsidiary of Cablevision, owns the cable channels AMC, WE,

Independent Film Channel, Voom HD Networks, Fuse TV, News 12, the Sundance Channel, and several others. It also owns the Video on Demand networks, lifeskool, and sportskool. With that roster of venues, it is evident that they have a full menu of offerings when it comes to the demographics and information and entertainment venue requirements of advertisers. But they too are faced with the challenges of the media ecology and the demands of the marketplace to prove superiority over like competitors. To do that, Brand Keys, Inc. and Rainbow Media designed a 3-phase research program to identify the following three sets of measures:

1. The levels of engagement that would result from a brand's advertising on a number of appropriate cable networks, *i.e.,* were the brand's values reinforced, unaffected, or degraded by their prospective appearance on one cable network or another?

2. The brand advertising's subsequent performance via a traditional captive-audience advertising test on measures of *category-aided advertising awareness, overall brand imagery ratings,* and *top-2 box purchase intent,* and

3. The real, in-market behavior of target consumers who had been exposed to the advertising on one cable network versus another in the captive-audience test.

PHASE ONE: ENGAGEMENT LEVELS OF VARIOUS CABLE NETWORKS

Telephone interviews were conducted nationally among the target audiences for a number of product and service categories. Appropriately screened respondents included demographically and behaviorally suitable prospects: women 25 to 59 years of age who shopped at one or more of the Discount Retailers included in the survey, two or more times a month, who regularly watched or were top-2 box familiar with the cable networks included in the study. They assessed the following phase one survey variables:

- The Ideal Discount Retailer,

- The Target brand (among other brands in the category) *as a stand-alone entity, i.e.,* on the basis of the respondents' current levels of exposure and knowledge of the brand and *not* in the context of any particular media vehicle,

- Category attributes, benefits, and values, and

- The Target brand *within* the context of a number of cable networks appropriate for the brand, *i.e.,* "Target advertised on WE."

Weighted averages of the Target brand, absent any media affiliation, and the brand advertised on various cable networks were calculated.

As a reminder to the reader, engagement results are identified on the basis of whether a brand's advertising on one cable network or another significantly increased the levels of brand equity for the brand. It is designed to answer this critical question:

Is the brand's ability as a stand-alone entity, and its ability to meet or exceed consumer expectations for the category, helped, hurt, or left alone by choosing to advertise on one appropriate cable network versus another equally appropriate cable network?

We segmented them into statistically-defined groups called "High Engagement Media," "Neutral Engagement Media," or "Negative Engagement Media." For the purpose of illustrating how these predictive results affect real consumer perceptions of the brand and how they actually play out in the real marketplace, we have selected one cable network from each segment, as follows:

Table 4.1
B2ME Scores For Select Cable Networks

High Engagement Media	
Target As Advertised on WE	117
Neutral Engagement Media	
Target	**109**
Target As Advertised on Oxygen	106
Negative Engagement Media	
Target As Advertised on Soapnet	100

PHASE TWO: HOW BRAND ADVERTISING CORRELATED WITH ENGAGEMENT METRICS

To determine the actual effects of a Target commercial placed on each of the three selected cable networks, standard captive audience tests were conducted in New York, Chicago, and Kansas City.

Respondents were identically screened as those in phase one and were exposed to the same 3-commercial "pod" (one of which was for Target) seamlessly inserted into the 11-12 minute point in the actual shows that were running on the same day at the same time period for each of the 3 cable networks. Keep in mind that any of these cable networks or specific shows would have provided Target with access to an audience comprised of both customers and prospects.

One hundred and fifty respondents (fifty in each of the three cities) were exposed to a single half-hour of programming for one of the cable shows listed above, so geographical location and any effects that might be due to any Discount Retailer preferences were obviated.

After viewing, they were then asked to respond to a series of traditional captive audience test questions related to category-aided advertising awareness for the three commercials that had run, which included automobile, discount retailer, and skin cream commercials. When the appropriate time in the question sequence came, they were asked to rate "Target in the commercial you just watched on (CABLE NETWORK NAME)" on a 1-to-7 scale, where "1" was poor and "7" was superior, and to respond to a standard, 5-box purchase interest question.

This was done for all three cable networks. Results were as follows:

Table 4.2
Results of Captive Audience Test

	Target B2ME Score	*Category-Aided Ad Awareness*	*Brand Imagery (1-7)*	*Top-2 Box Purchase Intent*
Target As Advertised on WE	117	65%	6.5	40%
Target As Advertised on Oxygen	106	58%	5.45	35%
Target As Advertised on Soapnet	100	42%	5.8	36%
Correlations		0.924	0.77	0.86

PHASE THREE: HOW IN-MARKET BEHAVIOR CORRELATED WITH ENGAGEMENT METRICS

We believe that it is axiomatic that any advertisement that has more attention paid to it, where the brand is thought of better after viewers have been exposed to it, and where the likelihood of purchasing the advertised brand is increased, has pretty much done its job. And while real engagement metrics always correlate highly with those measures, we are also mindful of the maxim; "a day in the marketplace is worth a month in the laboratory." Or a captive audience amphitheatre.

So instead of resting only on our correlations, respondents were also asked to keep a shopping diary regarding the frequency and size of purchases in two of the categories that appeared in the commercials (skin cream and discount retailers) for a 3-week period of time. So, what happened in the real world? The overall results for discount retailers were as follows:

Table 4.3
In-Market Behavior

Audience	Target B2ME Score	Average # of Visits (over 3 weeks)	Average $ Spend per Visit
Individuals who saw Target on WE	117	3.9	$28.13
Individuals who saw Target on Oxygen	106	3.7	$20.27
Individuals who saw Target on Soapnet	100	2.8	$21.91
Correlations		0.867	0.850

And the relationship between Brand-to-Media Engagement (B2ME) scores and market activity? Superior correlations of 0.867 with the average number of visits to Target stores and 0.850 for the average dollar spend per visit conclusively demonstrates the ability of these metrics to predicatively measure engagement. This is true as it relates to media selection as well as the ability to facilitate positive and profitable consumer behavior toward a brand. Thus the results indisputably prove that it is possible to predictively measure how to better engage an audience.

But it doesn't have to stop there. Once a media option is identified, there are engagement optimization assessments that can help influence the power of your communications and amplify your budget allocations.

POSITION, POSITION, POSITION

We've all heard the old joke that the three most-important things in retail success are "location, location, location." Well, just as retailers have long been willing to pay for "prime location," the same often holds true for magazine advertising.

But while retailers insist on calculating the return on their investment in terms of increased store traffic and sales, advertisers traditionally have paid a premium for a better "position" in magazines without value-added proof, or at least no proof that correlates with sales. And as brands increasingly demand return-on-investment (ROI) metrics on their large advertising budgets, premiums on positions will need to be defensible or that revenue stream will quickly become a rock bed.

To help magazine advertisers measure the impact and return on their investment in the print medium, we set B2ME metrics to answer the position-to-ROI question. This critical research and its ROI implications demonstrate that there *is* now an easy way for a brand to determine "position effects" in magazines.

To assess the return-on-investment a particular magazine position might generate, Brand Keys took a new ad for Ralph Lauren's women's fragrance and tested it in eight positions in each of three magazines; *Cosmopolitan, Glamour,* and <u>*Vogue*</u>, among women, 25 to 40 years of age.

The positions included:

- Cover 2/Page 1
- Page 3

- 2nd Fragrance advertisement
- Table of Contents
- Editor's Letter
- "Beauty" Editorial
- The Horoscope
- Cover 3

We used Ralph Lauren because Lauren is a 'gold standard' fashion brand in our annual *Fashion Brands Loyalty Index* study, which gets reported in *Women's Wear Daily* each year. The Ralph Lauren brand has high awareness, is differentiated from the competition, has established real and resonating values with its target audiences, and there are no questions about the strategic and production quality of their advertising. Ralph Lauren brand equity, exclusive of any media or advertising, indexed at a 119, meaning consumers rate it 19 percent higher than the benchmark brand, and their overall brand image is superior, a 6.25 overall, as rated on a 1-to-7 scale on the following attributes: *Being a stylish fragrance, Right for me, Value for dollars*, and *Having a quality image*. At any rate, knowing these facts ahead of time obviates a lot of possible problems fashion brands generally face in any kind of advertising test.

So the question is, are positions worth the investment?

The answer is. . . it depends. It depends on the position, *and* on the particular magazine in which the ad runs.

Keep in mind that from a demographic and editorial environment perspective, all of these magazines are appropriate choices for the brand. But it also depends on the strategic rationale and imperative for running the ad. Brand Keys tested each position to determine which provided optimum awareness, increased levels of brand imagery, and purchase-intent.

As might be assumed, the *Cover 2/Page 1* ad position turned out to be worth the investment, generally speaking. But, interestingly, being adjacent to the *Table of Contents* provided an equal "lift" in ad awareness, brand image, and a willingness to purchase the product for themselves or as a gift.

But the "urban media myth" that position "up front" is better than buying the "back of the book" may be just that.

Our survey showed consumer reactions to the test ad were virtually the same whether the ad appeared on *Page 3,* within *"Beauty" Editorial,* or even adjacent to the *Horoscope* which was located way back in the triple digits.

Table 4.3
In-Market Behavior

Audience	Target B2ME Score	Average # of Visits (over 3 weeks)	Average $ Spend per Visit
Individuals who saw Target on WE	117	3.9	$28.13
Individuals who saw Target on Oxygen	106	3.7	$20.27
Individuals who saw Target on Soapnet	100	2.8	$21.91
Correlations		**0.867**	**0.850**

Table 4.5
Cosmopolitan

	B2ME Score	Proven Awareness	Brand Imagery (1-7)	Top-2 Box Purchase Intent
Cover 2/Page 1	130	11%	6.7	28%
Page 3	113	6%	6.3	18%
2nd Fragrance	129	9%	6.5	20%
Table of Contents	128	9%	6.5	23%
Editor's Letter	120	7%	6.4	19%
"Beauty" Editorial	120	5%	6.25	12%
Horoscope	113	3%	6.0	10%
Cover 3	127	10%	6.5	26%
Correlations		**0.90**	**0.88**	**0.80**

Table 4.6
Glamour

	B2ME Score	Proven Awareness	Brand Imagery (1-7)	Top-2 Box Purchase Intent
Cover 2/Page 1	128	10%	6.7	22%
Page 3	125	8%	6.6	21%
2nd Fragrance	126	8%	6.5	20%
Table of Contents	129	9%	6.6	23%
Editor's Letter	110	3%	6.3	14%
"Beauty" Editorial	112	4%	6.5	15%
Horoscope	120	6%	6.4	13%
Cover 3	115	7%	6.6	20%
Correlations		**0.93**	**0.65**	**0.76**

Being the *2nd Fragrance* ad in the book, *or* advertising on *Cover 3,* resulted in positive effects in two of the three magazines. Being adjacent to the *Editor's Letter* added value in only one of the magazines, telling us that that the environment of the magazine itself is important too.

We know from previous B2ME research that the media environment can either enhance or detract from an advertised brand's values. We also know that there's a direct correlation to the attention a reader will pay to the ad and how they feel about the brand and at what level they'd consider purchasing the advertised brand. That being the case, it's inevitable that different brands and different positions in different magazines will produce different ROI patterns.

Unfortunately, you can't generalize what works for Ralph Lauren to other brands. Assessments of other brands would, naturally, deliver other, different brand-specific findings and insights. But the critical research and ROI implications of the study demonstrate that there is now an easy way to determine "position effects" in magazines, and lets brands decide for themselves whether or not premium pricing is providing premium engagement.

That means, using this method, that the media can now actually certify the positive effects of select positions. Advertisers can know exactly what value they will receive for their media spend, and can know this *before* spending their budgets — making this kind of engagement research the most valuable piece of real estate on this game board.

THE KEYHOLE:
PEEKING AT 21ST CENTURY BRANDS:

February 27, 2006

AND THE OSCAR FOR ENGAGEMENT GOES TO.

I hope that some of you are going to watch the 78th Academy Awards next Sunday because audience ratings have not been very kind to the Oscars in recent years. The ratings were down 21% in 2004, and declined even further in 2005. Switching dates because of the Winter Olympics can't have helped.

The Academy of Motion Picture Arts and Sciences have made efforts to rebuild the audience, but as they don't directly control the movies that get produced, and have only limited influence on the ones that get nominated, they end up placing the burden on engaging an audience on the host.

Last year it was, if you remember, Chris Rock. But he didn't seem to help very much. Billy Crystal has done it a number of times, and people absolutely love him and his opening musical numbers. But interestingly, if you check the actual viewership numbers, you'll find that when Crystal was host he had the highest — and the lowest — audience numbers measured over the past ten years.

Anyway, this year the Academy turned to Jon Stewart, host of Comedy Central's award-winning fake news program *The Daily Show*. When it was announced that he was selected to host the awards, he said, "As a performer, I'm truly honored to be hosting the show, although as an avid watcher of the Oscars, I can't help but be a little disappointed with the choice." Funny guy.

All of which may just point out the validity of the statement that "entertaining is not the same thing as engaging," a fact that a large number of advertisers and branded entertainment consumers might well take to heart.

ABC sold all of its inventory for the awards telecast, with 30-second spots costing an average of $1.7 million, so you've got to figure that advertisers are looking for some sense of return on a pretty big investment. And to that end, Brand Keys conducted the 1st Academy Awards Engagement Survey®.

The survey was conducted among 1,000 men and women, 18 to 59 years of age, who expressed a top-box intention to watch the March 5th broadcast.

Creative "reviews" are interesting, but more and more, clients are revisiting the question of seeing a return on their investment. Anyway, the *Academy Awards Engagement Survey*, like the Brand Keys *Customer Loyalty Index*, was conducted expressly to tease out respondents true behaviors. The process quantifies the levels of engagement created by the media environment and advertised brand — the equity increase (or decrease) resulting from an advertising effort on a particular show like the Academy Awards. It reports the "return" or "loss" from the advertising effort itself. The engagement metrics were indexed to allow for cross-category brand comparisons and provide measures generalizable at the 95% confidence level.

The results? Only 25% of the brands advertising on the Academy Awards showed increased levels of brand equity. An increase in brand equity always results in increased engagement. That means that viewers will pay more attention to the advertising, think better of the brand, and actually go out and buy the advertised product.

The Brand Keys assessments provide a predictive measure of an ad's return, no matter how "creative" the advertising. Advertising is something more than just seeing — even liking — the commercial. It's creating an emotional bond between the product and the viewer. The ads are not seen in a vacuum so the media environment in which you place them can help or hurt.

And the envelope, please. The awards for real Consumer Engagement goes to: L'Oreal, Cadillac, American Express, and Coke. We suppose the other brands will just have to be content with knowing their ads ran, a number of eyeballs watched, and they reached their demographics.

Time magazine names Stewart one of its most influential people of 2005 so it will be interesting to see if Stewart can influence the ratings. But to paraphrase actor Edmund Gwenn, these days it may just be a case where comedy is easy and engagement is difficult.

1 year later. . .

Preliminary Nielsen estimates showed this year's Oscar telecast 20% below last year's. Its 21.9 household rating was considerably below the 2003 Academy Awards telecast, which set the low-water mark for viewership of these types of shows.

5

Navigating in a Media Monsoon: How to Buy Media in the 21st Century

Movement is not an adequate substitution for action.

Raymond Chandler

Can we agree that everyone pretty much has the locating-my-audience-demographic thing down? Is there really any difficulty locating your target audience? We know more today about the consumer than ever before and media, like medicine, has become more specialized. And that specialization has not made media planning or buying easier. In fact, just the opposite has happened. With so many media platforms able to supply demographic information that matches up with the target audience a brand is trying to reach, how does the media buyer know how to best allocate resources for true, optimized marketplace effects? Combine that reality with the proliferation of media touch points available to the advertisers — again, all with tidy demographic statistics — and the task of media evaluation suddenly makes casting chicken bones into the sand look like solid research.

And, just to add one more dust devil, how does the buyer know *how* the various media platforms are integrating into the lives of real consumers? Is it any wonder that media buyers leave their jobs in search of something with less risk, like say, snake charming?

There are, of course, the traditional fall-backs like "time spent." But today, media buyers have to deal with the conundrum of simultaneous media consumption and fragmented "time spent." Today, more than 75 percent of consumers spend time using other media like newspapers or going online while watching TV. And as generations of new consumers come into the market, they are more visually and brand literate, so we can only expect simultaneous consumption to increase.

One could — as some do — assess media on the basis of some form of cross-category indicator, like "trust" or "confidence," and evaluate media on the basis of it possessing some kind of value-based editorial environment. Here, the theory goes, if the medium is regarded as "trustworthy," for example, your brand will be too if you advertise in a "trustworthy" venue. Practitioners of this philosophy think of it as a kind of media value "halo effect." This approach has been called "Vaudeville Research," because it's only effective if you buy the premise — then you buy the bit! And anyway, relying on some assessment mechanism based on identifying media touch points that consumers love or trust is less than helpful when what you really want to know is what's going to happen once the ad runs. After it runs it is just plain history. And you know what they say about that: history is a wonderful thing because it lets you recognize a mistake when you make it again. One can only suppose that there is some solace in the fact that the demographics were correct.

That makes engagement the real differentiator.

To be predictive, real engagement must be something more than easily-ascribed, image-based, possible "halo effects." Look at how many "High Fashion" magazines there are and how some campaigns do better in one magazine than another. Remember the multi-page spread WalMart ran in *Vogue*? How much did they benefit from *Vogue's* unquestionable *haute couture* values? Where was the halo effect then? Nothing — not even a glow. And, while values are, of course, important, those "indicator" lists tend to be restricted to a very short-list of values and are also very general. So, matching brands and the advertisements for those brands to media platforms and venues that have been rated in certain ways neither guarantees that the brand's values will be enhanced nor that customers will be engaged.

An engagement-based approach eliminates the issues regarding "time spent" and the uncertain values attributed to a particular medium over and above the actual editorial environment. Those aspects may be useful when it comes to having a better understanding regarding *how* media dollars should be allocated, but real engagement measures allow marketers to better understand the tangible effects on the brand that will be engendered by actual media consumption. That's true whether you are looking at a single-serve medium or in cross-media servings.

That means the buyer is finally able to create a predictive media plan based on real marketplace effects, not media-kit assertions and data base assumptions. And media platforms can now prove their right to have a preferred place at the buying table by demonstrating the impact they have on engagement.

As we discussed in Chapter 3, authentic engagement output always provides an identification of the category drivers that define *how* the target audience views the category, compares brand offerings, and, ultimately, how consumers will *behave* in the marketplace. But for media planning and media platform assessments, it's a secondary output-element that is mission critical: the identification of the percent-contribution made to engagement, loyalty, and sales by *any* marketing element or variable included in the assessment. This can include *any* consumer or category attribute, benefit, or value, not limited to a research supplier fixed list of pre-defined and pre-determined values that the brand is loathe to walk away from because they come with an "average" — the only measurement the brand has to imagine success or failure, however irrelevant. In these days of creeping commoditization and consumer cleverness, all brands need the flexibility to assess whatever attributes, benefits, and values (ABVs) the brand might wish to own, leverage, or acquire.

Serendipitously, the process can also assess the percent-contribution of the various *media touch points and platforms* and identify to what degree they will contribute to — and facilitate — engagement within the category. Keep in mind that these assessments describe how target audiences consume media and — as category realities differ — will vary from category-to-category.

The next chart is an example of engagement-based, touch point assessments. It examines twenty-six above-the-line, below-the-line, and new media touch points that *might* conceivably be used by a financial services brand. This is an aggregate assessment to give an overall "feel" for the concept, approach, and output. This includes Banks, Credit Cards, Mutual Funds, Online Brokers, and Insurance Companies, so note that the specific percent-contributions will vary somewhat from category-to-category. Remember, while they may all be financially-based, and "trust" or "confidence" may be desired and even necessary, consumers *don't* buy Mutual Funds they way they sign up for a Credit Card or a checking account. And the media used to present the brand messages can have significant influence over whether your brand equity is enhanced or not — and whether they sign with you or your competitor.

Table 5.1
Percent-Contribution of Various Advertising Media Touch Points:
Financial Services Category

TV Broadcast	10%	*TIVO*	3%
TV Cable	10%	*Cell Phone*	2%
Direct Mail	9%	*Email Advertising*	2%
Article about Product	8%	*Instant Messenger*	2%
Word of Mouth	7%	*Outdoor Billboard*	2%
Radio	6%	*PDA*	2%
ISP/Search Engines	5%	*Satellite Radio*	2%
Magazines	5%	*Web Radio*	2%
Newspaper Insert	5%	*MP3 Player*	1%
Newspapers	4%	*Picture Phone*	1%
At Retail	3%	*Text Message*	1%
In-Store Promotion	3%	*Video Games*	1%
Internet Advertising	3%	*Yellow Pages*	1%

So, given these findings, where would you invest your marketing dollars? You need to keep in mind that these assessments are category-focused and will change category-to-category. You also need to remember that these assessments are not inert. They will — just like all loyalty and engagement assessments — change as the categories, and brands, and consumers change and adapt to the new media ecology and new brand values.

And while Video Games only make a one percent contribution to engagement and loyalty in the Financial Services category, it is far more effectual in, for example, the Political Arena. There the same media touch point makes nearly an eight percent contribution. Interesting, but not practical? But just weeks before the 2008 Presidential elections, video gamers playing "Burnout Paradise" who were connected to the Internet were also connected to an in-game system that allowed real life sponsors to place advertisements on virtual billboards in the game's digital world. And Barack Obama's presidential campaign purchased ads to run in ten battleground states for the Xbox 360® version of the game — the most popular among men, 16 to 30 years of age — right up to Election Day.

While absolutely predictive of how hard the media will work in a particular category, this is limited to a category perspective. It is a 10,000-foot view, and while useful, it is isolated from the brand, which should be the ultimate beneficiary of the marketing exercise. A brand perspective is going to be more helpful and laser-like and is always going to correlate to the positive outcomes you're hoping for from your efforts: increased attention paid to your message, better brand imagery, higher propensity to buy you and not your competitor, higher actual sales, and loyalty. The following section of this chapter not only examines cross-media consumption effects, but also provides a single, category-specific touch point assessment as well.

WELCOME TO THE MEDIA ECOLOGY

Forty years ago, New York University professor Neil Postman, a media theorist and cultural critic, predicted the coming of what he termed a "media ecology." Postman noted, "Media ecology looks into the matter of how media of communication affect human perception, understanding, feeling and value," which astoundingly seems to reflect the concerns modern marketers are faced with today regarding integrated and cross-media utilization.

A decade later, communications theorist Marshall McLuhan further observed that a "media ecology means arranging various media to help each other. . . to buttress one medium with another," which sounds astonishingly like the current problem marketers face regarding integrated media planning and the measurement of cross-media consumption effects.

One can argue about the precise date that this media ecology finally arrived in its full-blown complexity. We peg it around 1985. But what is incontrovertible is that a real, 21st century media ecology, that is to say, an environment where consumers are virtually cocooned by — or have access to — media of one sort or another 24/7/365, has arrived. It goes without saying that media planning for this environment is more complex than ever before. And, as planning complexity cannot be denied, it is critical that marketers are able to measure their brand's integrated and cross-media consumed interaction in this "ecology." More importantly, perhaps, the undeniable existence of the media ecology makes the assessment of its effects on consumer engagement, brand development, and sales all the more necessary.

Yes, it is undeniable that some media formats are more practicable. Others are more "cost-effective." Each touch point argues that they incorporate a unique set and subset of values, nuances, and capabilities to communicate, inform, and persuade. And — based upon our predictive Brand-to-Media Engagement (B2ME) metrics — some *are* actually more efficacious for certain categories and brands than others. We also recognize that embracing more and different media touch points *theoretically* optimizes the opportunity the brand has to be exposed to the target consumer, since any one consumer uses different forms of media at different times. But that being the case, reasonable people might ask that *if* each medium has its strengths, and *if* a combination of media has even greater potency, won't the brand with the most touch points win?

No — this is not a simple more-is-better model. The Cross-Media Engagement (XME) assessment answers that question by demonstrating the effects cross-media consumption has on brand engagement levels — both positive *and* negative — as well as consumer behavior in the marketplace. More importantly, it provides predictive measures as to the effects integrated media can create as well as the in-market behavior that cross-media consumption will generate.

THE XME MODEL

The XME model is an engagement-based assessment that "fuses" emotional and rational values that govern brand engagement and loyalty, identifies the category drivers, and calculates the percent-contribution made to engagement, loyalty, and sales by *any* marketing element or variable. This includes *media vehicles.*

And, while strategic brand planning and cross-media consumption are not mutually exclusive, or shouldn't be, in this case, the XME model was created to assess the impact of media platforms and combinations on engagement. The following research effort measures twenty-six individual media touch points that marketers might have conceivably used to engage and persuade consumers to the brand's particular point-of-view — individually and in combination with one another. The category: Moisturizing Bar Soap.

The XME approach allows marketers to better understand media integration and consumption. Through the diagnostics, marketers can not only identify the impact media has on the success of a brand when used together, but also how — and in what way — the media combinations work from a strategic brand perspective. Media can then be allocated on a more synergistic and efficient basis, which, in a more complex marketplace, is more and more critical to the success of a brand.

INTEGRATED PLANNING AND CROSS-MEDIA CONSUMPTION

The XME survey was conducted in three phases:

- Phase one was conducted to identify a brand engagement benchmark for the Dove® brand as well as the predictive metrics of the percent-contribution to engagement of the twenty-six individual media touch points.

- Phase two identified measurable cross-media consumption segments, the effects this consumption had on the Dove brand equity, and actual purchase levels.

- Phase three determined the summative, per-cent-contribution made by each of the cross-media consumption groupings identified in phase two. That is to say, if TV made an 18 percent contribution and Magazines made an eight percent contribution, a segment of consumers exposed to advertising via TV *and* Magazines were assigned a XME contribution of 26 percent. These predictive XME percent-contributions were then correlated to self-reported, past 60-day purchases of Dove moisturizing soap.

PHASE ONE: THE DOVE BENCHMARK AND INTEGRATED MEDIA VALUES

Two hundred interviews were conducted with exclusive Dove and Ivory moisturizing soap users. All had purchased their brand in the past 60 days. All respondents assessed the Ideal Moisturizing Bar Soap, twenty category attributes, benefits, and values, and the twenty-six media touch points. Respondents assessed only the brand they used exclusively, the Dove brand or the Ivory brand.

Thus, the Ideal provides us with a description of the ultimate "moisturizing bar soap" for the Total Audience, while the brand assessments measure how the brand-exclusive users see their preferred brand in terms of how well it meets or, sometimes, even exceeds their conception of the Ideal.

The combined audience Ideal Moisturizing Soap appears in Figure 5.1. As a reminder, category drivers are listed in order of importance from left to right, and the indexed heights of the bars describe the levels of expectations consumers hold for each of the drivers.

The higher the expectations, the greater the potential for brand differentiation.

Pro forma brand engagement assessments provide the percent-contribution that each individual attribute, benefit, and value makes to engagement and loyalty. In this case, that also included the twenty-six media touch points that were to be used in configuring some integrated media plan for the brand. The result of that analysis will be discussed and utilized in phase three.

Engagement assessments for the Ideal and the brands were as follows:

Figure 5.1
Moisturizing Soap Brands vs. Ideal

A weighted average of the brand-specific assessments are calculated and provides an overall Brand Equity Index score. In this case, Dove was calculated to be 113, which, for cross-media consumption purposes, represents the Brand Engagement Benchmark. This benchmark signifies the brand *in toto;* everything the consumer has seen, heard, or experienced about the brand, and in this moment in time, absent of any media context.

PHASE TWO: CAPTURING CROSS-MEDIA CONSUMPTION AND RATING THE BRAND

Phase two was conducted among a matched sample of 2,000 exclusive Dove users who had purchased the brand in the past 60 days.

Respondents were asked to self-report on which of the twenty-six media touch points they had "seen Dove advertising in the past 60 days," and to rate the "Dove brand they had seen advertised." By collecting the assessments in this manner, we felt that this would capture the gestalt of the brand advertising to which they had been exposed. Their options included the following:

Table 5.2
Media Touch Points

Article about Product	MP3 Player	Search Engines
At Retail	Newspaper Insert	Sponsorships
Cell Phone	Newspapers	Text Message
Direct Mail	Outdoor Billboard	TIVO
Email Advertising	Out Of Home Digital	TV Broadcast
Instant Messenger	PDA	TV Cable
In-Store Promotion	Picture Phone	Video Games
Internet Advertising	Promotions	Web Radio
ISP	Radio	Word of Mouth
Magazines	Satellite Radio	Yellow Pages

Respondents were also asked to indicate how many bars of soap they had purchased in the same 60-day time period.

It should come as no surprise that given the current media ecology and myriad ways in which consumers use media — and the more numerous and complex ways in which advertisers integrate these touch points into their media plans — segments large enough to provide generalizable samples of "one-off" touch points were difficult to come by.

In fact, only one such segment revealed itself, and that was magazines.

"Television" has been included as a "one-off" segment not only because it is an essential and most voluminous medium, but because it is also generally the medium that accounts for the "lion's share" of major brands' budgets. What's more, it *always* seems to account for the medium with the largest "time spent," at least among an audience buying moisturizing soap. Those points conceded, the paucity of consumer segments reporting only one medium as the place they had "seen Dove advertising in the past 60 days," required us to combine both "broadcast" and "cable" to create a "TV Only" segment.

Thus, the following eleven consumption segments with large enough user segments *i.e.,* 150+ respondents, were revealed:

Table 5.3
Cross Media Consumption Segments

TV Only (Broadcast & Cable)	TV + Word of Mouth	Magazines Only
TV + Magazines	TV + Word of Mouth +ISP	Magazines + Word of Mouth
TV + Magazines + Newspaper Insert	TV + Word of Mouth + ISP + Article	Magazines + Word of Mouth + ISP
	TV + Word of Mouth + ISP + At Retail	
	TV + Word of Mouth + Magazines	

Using real engagement metrics allows us to calculate the impact that these integrated media segments had on brand equity. It is important to note that this phase of the research was an historical view — an understanding of what happened after the fact.

As the purpose of these engagement assessments is to offer clients *predictive* leading-indicator metrics and not lagging indicators, this output is most important when compared to the predictive measures calculated in phase one — especially as they correlate with sales. The excellent correlations of our phase one predictive metrics with the historical metrics of phase two are reported out in phase three.

The brand engagement metrics were used to identify the media consumption segments as having produced "an increased level of brand equity for the advertised brand." In this instance it classifies the media effort as a "High

Engagement Brand Enhancer." Based on all previous work in this area, that means the effort should correlate with higher degrees of positive attitudes and, more importantly, positive in-market behavior toward the advertised brand.

Media consumption or marketing efforts or even individual media vehicles can be classified in two other ways. Firstly, as producing "Neutral" levels of engagement, indicating that the effort did not significantly reinforce brand values to a degree that consumers felt the brand better met or exceeded their conception of the category Ideal. And, secondly, engendering "Negative" levels of engagement, where brand values are actually degraded by the media environment, no matter how appropriate or available that venue seems to be.

The effects to the Dove brand equity — on the basis of the reported cross-media exposure to the Dove advertising — were:

Table 5.4
Brand Enhancers for Dove

High Engagement

TV + Word of Mouth + ISP + Article	137
TV + Word of Mouth + ISP	133
TV + Word of Mouth + Magazines	133
Magazines + Word of Mouth + ISP	132
TV + Word of Mouth + ISP + At Retail	130
TV + Word of Mouth	129
Magazines + Word of Mouth	128
TV + Magazines + Newspaper Insert	126
TV Magazines	125

Neutral Engagement

TV (Broadcast & Cable Only)	120
Magazines Only	118
Dove	*113*

It is interesting to note that the two media that normally account for the most time-spent and/or larger percentage(s) of the media budget — TV and magazines — while not degrading brand values, did *not* produce significant levels of brand engagement when "consumed" on their own.

But, nine of the cross-media consumption segments *did* produce significantly higher engagement for the Dove brand. Examined on a cross-media consumption basis, seven of these segments included TV and five included magazines. Only three of the segments included both TV and magazines.

PHASE THREE: XME VALUES CORRELATED TO BRAND EQUITY AND TO SALES

Earlier in this chapter we noted that on a *pro forma* basis, brand engagement output provides the percent-of-contribution that each variable included in the assessment ultimately makes to engagement and loyalty. In this particular study that included the twenty-six possible media touch points that Dove might have conceivably used in the marketing of their brand.

Keeping in mind that these assessments describe how target audiences consume media and will vary from category-to-category, the results of that analysis for the "Moisturizing Bar Soap" category were found to be as follows:

Table 5.5
Contributions of Various Media Touch Points:
Moisturizing Bar Soap

Word of Mouth	12%	Internet Advertising	2%
ISP/ Search Engines	11%	Newspapers	2%
Article about Product	10%	Text Message	2%
TV Cable	10%	Cell Phone	.5%
Magazines	8%	MP3 Player	.5%
TV Broadcast	8%	PDA	.5%
In-Store Promotion	7%	Picture Phone	.5%
At Retail	5%	Radio	.5%
Direct Mail	5%	Satellite Radio	.5%
Outdoor Billboard	5%	TIVO	.5%
Newspaper Insert	4%	Video Games	.5%
Email Advertising	2%	Web Radio	.5%
Instant Messenger	2%	Yellow Pages	.5%

Summative calculations of percent-of-contribution were made for each of the media consumption segments identified in phase two of the research.

Table 5.6
Summative Media Contribution

Article about
At Retail
Cell Phone
Direct Mail
Email
Instant
In-Store
Internet
ISP/Search
Magazines
MP3 Player
Newspapers
Outdoor

PDA
Picture Phone
Radio
Satellite Radio
Text Message
TIVO
TV Broadcast
TV Cable
Video Games
Web Radio
Word of Mouth
Yellow Pages

Cross-Media	Percent Contribution
Magazines Only	8%
TV (Broadcast & Cable)	18%
TV + Magazines	26%
TV + Magazines + Newspaper Insert	30%
Magazines + Word of Mouth	20%
TV + Word of Mouth	30%
TV + Word of Mouth + ISP + At Retail	51%
Magazines + Word of Mouth + ISP	31%
TV + Word of Mouth + ISP	38%
TV + Word of Mouth + Magazines	72%
TV + Word of Mouth + ISP + Article	51%

This portion of the survey analysis also included the calculation of correlations for cross-media consumption values with engagement effects to the brand *and* with reported purchases.

The correlation between percent of "lift" to brand engagement based on cross-media consumption and the XME summative calculations of percent-of-contribution made by the cross-media groupings was found to be 0.769.

Table 5.7
Engagement Lift to Brand Equity

Cross-Media Consumption Segments	"Lift" to Brand Equity	Media Percent - Contribution to Engagement & Loyalty: Ideal
	(Phase II)	(Phase I)
Magazines Only	21%	8%
TV (Broadcast & Cable) Only	29%	18%
TV + Magazines	50%	26%
TV + Magazines + Newspaper Insert	54%	30%
Magazines + Word of Mouth	63%	20%
TV + Word of Mouth	67%	30%
TV + Word of Mouth + ISP + At Retail	71%	51%
Magazines + Word of Mouth + ISP	79%	31%
TV + Word of Mouth + ISP	83%	38%
TV + Word of Mouth + Magazine	83%	72%
TV + Word of Mouth + ISP + Article	100%	51%

Next, we calculated the correlation between XME summative calculations of percent-of-contribution made by the cross-media groupings and the average past 60-day purchases of Dove moisturizing bar soap.

Table 5.8
Actual Purchase

Cross-Media Consumption Segments	Summative Media Percent Contribution	Average 60-Day Purchase (# of bars)
Magazines Only	8%	5
TV (Broadcast & Cable) Only	18%	8
TV + Magazines	26%	8
TV + Magazines + Newspaper Insert	30%	10
Magazines + Word of Mouth	20%	5
TV + Word of Mouth	30%	7
TV + Word of Mouth + ISP + At Retail	51%	12
Magazines + Word of Mouth + ISP	31%	8
TV + Word of Mouth + ISP	38%	9
TV + Word of Mouth + Magazines	72%	11
TV + Word of Mouth + ISP + Article	51%	15

The correlation between these two measures was 0.779.

We find these correlations — beyond their statistical potency — heartening because while the values were calculated on the basis of the "Ideal Moisturizing Soap," it is clear that with some fine-tuning it can be used to create a Dove-specific media-engagement value equation. And, we believe that it is fair to say that these calculations, with certainty, prove the efficacy of engagement-based cross-media consumption and integrated media measures.

In the spirit of full disclosure, the results of a correlation between the summative percent-of-contributions made by the cross-media groupings and *how* Unilever actually allocated their budget dollars was less impressive. There we only had a correlation of 0.298. But this did not come as a total surprise given the fact that "allocation" and "consumption" are two different activities. Costs related to purchasing TV time is generally far more expensive than, say, web site or Public Relations or Word-of-Mouth activities.

AN ENGAGEMENT EXTRA: SELECTING MEDIA ON THE BASIS OF A BRAND'S STRATEGIC NEEDS

The XME assessment not only provides high correlations that predictively identify how well cross-media consumption reinforces a brand's values, but its diagnostics identify *which* of the four category drivers of engagement and loyalty are being most-highly influenced by the "insertion" of the brand into one media option versus another.

In this study, these measures show the difference between the brand benchmark and the "Dove brand seen advertised" for each of the cross-media consumption segments. The following is an example of a diagnostic chart that indicates the effects for the TV Only (Broadcast and Cable) segment and the integrated TV + Word-of-Mouth + ISP + Article cross-media consumption segment.

Figure 5.2
Effects for TV (Broadcast and Cable) Only and TV + Word of Mouth + ISP + Article

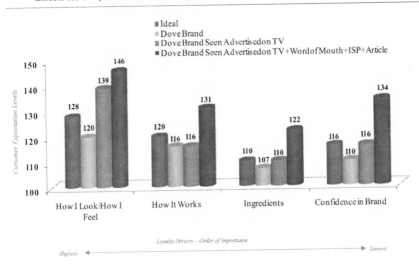

Note that among the 'TV Only' segment, positive strategic effects show up as primarily influencing only one category driver, *How I Look/How I Feel.* But among the 'TV +' cross-media consumption segment, significant and positive effects show up in *all four* of the category drivers that influence engagement, loyalty, and product purchase.

With information like this for each integrated media combination and each cross-media consumption segment anticipated, it is actually possible to select media for a campaign on the basis of which set of options will best reinforce the brand on the basis of specific copy and engagement objectives.

This assessment can, of course, be conducted on specific programs as well, *i.e., Desperate Housewives* versus *The View,* to pick the right option for your brand. You need to be able to do this because the reality is that many programs will be right for your brand. But you will fail to maximize the effects of your efforts if you only buy "right" — meaning the program possesses a reasonable editorial environment and a large enough audience made up of the demographics against which you market. Today you need more.

Decision making about which show to place your advertising was far easier before the advent of cable and satellite TV, let alone computers and downloadable cell phones. What was once a decision to advertise on one show among the four or five that were running Monday night at 8:00, has morphed into a choice of nearly a thousand channels and — reasonably speaking — 20 to 30 perfectly "right" programs to choose from on that day in that time period.

Want to play media planner? Try your hand to matching the brands in Table 5.9 to the best show based — not strictly on demographics — but on which offers the maximum level of engagement.

Table 5.9
Engagement-Based Media Planning

1. 60 Minutes	A. McDonald's
2. Gossip Girl	B. Swiffer
3. CSI	C. eHarmony.com
4. House	D. Allstate Insurance
5. Monday Night Football	E. Fidelity Investments
6. Law and Order	F. Red Bull
7. Monk	G. Charles Schwab
8. NASCAR	H. Cadillac
9. The Closer	I. L'Oreal
10. Two and a Half Men	J. Miller Beer

Answers: 1-H, 2-F, 3-E, 4-G, 5-A, 6-J, 7-B, 8-C, 9-D, 10-I

Engagement-based media planning like this allows for more efficient and optimized planning for your brand. It is an adjunct to traditional media planning — albeit more laser targeted — and it can be done *before* spending your money!

HIGH EXPECTATIONS FOR ENGAGEMENT

At no time in post-modern marketing has the need to possess a consumer-centric measure of integrated media and cross-media consumption been so great. And while we have colleagues who publicly declare that it is impossible to measure integrated communications, we believe that the XME approach successfully puts an end to that misimpression.

The XME model explains how and in what ways media combinations work, and does so from both a behavioral (*i.e.,* product purchase) *and* attitudinal (*i.e.,* brand engagement) basis. The diagnostics make it possible to select media on the basis of which sets of integrated options will best *reinforce* the brand — based on category imperatives, specific copy objectives, or engagement goals.

The ability to do all this corroborates two marketing paradigm shifts. First, today advertising has become less about the character of the products to be consumed and more about the character of the consumers of the products, and, perhaps more particularly, the combinations of media they consume. And second, anyone who has been paying attention to the changes in the media ecology knows that the advent of new technologies involves some sort of trade-off. Change in this ecology does not necessarily result in equilibrium and, depending upon the category, some platforms and venues become greater contributors than others. Marketers need to know that.

Utilizing the XME approach means that "consumption" and "contribution" *can* be identified, and media can then be allocated and integrated on a more synergistic, efficient, and consumer-centric basis. This also means that the conventional, multi-year, multi-million dollar Cross Media Optimization studies can be supplanted with predictive and cost-effective XME analyses. Instead of having reports that read, "and so when we added in this media, we got that," reports can state with certainty that "*if* you add this, you'll get this." And given the current trends, it is certain that the ability to do that will become more and more critical to the success — and profitability — of a brand.

THE KEYHOLE:
PEEKING AT 21ˢᵀ CENTURY BRANDS:

May 15, 2007

UPFRONT HEADACHES

Expanding the revolt started last year when J&J and Coke pulled out of the TV upfront, half-billion-dollar big spender Unilever is re-evaluating its position too. Laura Klauberg, VP Media for Unilever has noted that the company is "weighing all our options in the upfront. . . Clearly, the market has changed a lot." Unilever cited difficulties of making upfront buys in advance of its calendar fiscal year and the fact that a good deal of marketing has become less TV-centric and more complex.

Well, we feel their pain and have, in fact, written about this for years. Yes, more complexity, and yes, more cross-media usage, and yes, newer opportunities appear weekly, but to paraphrase an old Wendy's commercial, "Where's the brand?"

Companies invest countless dollars in developing their "brands," but don't insert their brand's values into the media planning/buying process, planning by reach and frequency, or by what's new, different, and wonderful, or more socially-networked, or branded via entertainment vehicles. But that approach is flawed, because the media option's values may not reinforce the advertised brand's values. And that's what you need if you want to see increased levels of ad engagement and loyalty.

That being the case, Brand Keys developed Brand-to-Media Engagement (B2ME) assessments that measure the degree to which your media plan (above-the-line, below-the-line, and new media) reinforces your brand's values. In fact, current research reveals that worst case it can predict increased levels of brand awareness, engagement, and positive brand imagery, before your spend your money. Best case, it can actually predict sales resulting from your plan!

Comedian Fred Allen once offered up some funny ad statistics, quipping, "Advertising is 85% confusion and 15% commission," but the percentages have changed since that observation. If you want different numbers, here's some: with B2ME assessments you can generalize predictive media results at the 95% confidence level. Before you spend your money — upfront or otherwise!

And that's nothing to laugh at!

1 year, 1 month, and 2 weeks later. . .

TV Week reports: "Sales executives at the broadcast networks are grinning and cable network sales reps are rubbing their hands together. But the Buyers? Not so much." It seems that advertisers have moved to the upfront because they are concerned that if broadcast ratings continue to erode, prices will skyrocket again.

6

Broadcast + Digital = ?
Predictive Metrics Merge With
Profitability

All marriages are mixed marriages.

Chantel Silverstein

On the one hand, marketers and planners publicly declare that they are unable to measure integrated communications and cross-media consumption effects. Yet, on the other hand, they are equally quick, passionate, and vocal — and are virtually willing to swear — that myriad combinations of media entities will provide clients with value and values above and beyond just exposure to increasingly larger audiences.

And, as more touch points have inserted themselves into the marketing world, agencies and media planners have quickly jumped on those as well:

Video games are hot so let's see about getting your brand into one of those. Super Mario® sells really well. We can do something super with that!

People text message. Let's not wait for them to text the brand, we'll text them.

Look how many people have MP3 players. We can do something with that.

Well, you know what they say; music is the wine that fills the cup of silence, so let's add a couple of brand codas as well.

What was once one screen is now four, and they're all considered legitimate and fair game. And — costs and allocations not withstanding — to a large degree, each of these touch points are considered equal in the sight of the media planner. No, no. Don't deny it. Costs are different, but if you want it (or more likely, if your competitor is doing it) there's always some justification for including one platform versus the other. Not only that, they all have an equal opportunity of being included in the media plan.

We think it's fair to say that reasonable men (and women) can agree that the value of media entities (and combinations thereof) cannot and should not be defined solely by their size of the audience or their demographics. We should also be able to agree that different media formats are (or should be) uniquely differentiated by the quality of engagement levels that they can provide. And, their ability to enhance advertising effectiveness by association with one another. Take, for example, adding a digital platform to go along with traditional above and below-the-line media. You know, they're synergistic. They must be. That's how they got sold in the first place.

So, where are we? Well, with the proliferation of media choices and raised consumer expectations, consumers have more opportunities to engage with various media (or have media foisted upon them), as well as more control over their media experiences (or lack thereof, depending upon whether we are talking about TIVO, branded entertainment, or multi-screen exposures). For advertisers, increased media options have resulted in more "integrated" — and complex — market planning, which have resulted in the use of multiple media touch points. We've already discussed that issue. But the question still remains, what happens when you blend these media touch points?

If you are just optimizing the number of consumers who are *likely* to actually see or hear your message, well, OK. But these days, locating your audience isn't the problem, and hasn't been the problem for nearly 20 years. To be fair and balanced, most planners aren't defending their recommendations on just that basis. *Engaging* audiences is different. Getting them to go out and buy the product is very different still. Engaging consumers is more complex and prone to error, particularly in regards to integrated, multi-platform campaigns. And when you combine different media platforms, you are likely to get different results. But what? What will happen?

Without knowing whether you are meaningfully connecting a brand with consumers, advertising and marketing efforts are just forays of creative and communicative attempts aimed at what brands have identified as being "appropriate" audiences. The exposures — or, what might more accurately be described as "opportunities for exposure" — do not, unfortunately, guarantee that any positive behavior for the advertised brand will result from the exercise. And in light of advertisers and stockholders demanding accountability well beyond the metrics provided in the last century (and, sadly, into the new century), astute media planners and salespeople are seeing real Return-On-Investment as a way to differentiate themselves from the competition.

Now you *can* predict what *will* happen, *if* you measure engagement effects before you commit your marketing dollars. The model we use is an application of our Brand-to-Media Engagement assessments. As such, it can be extraordinarily useful when combining or "blending" media platforms. This more strategic and effective planning approach turns traditional "targets" into actual paying "customers." What should make marketers happy is that these assessments can be conducted *before* they spend their money.

What should make the media happy is that this is a major step forward for all media purveyors — both traditional and new — to differentiate themselves. Now they can actually *prove* superior utility individually and in combination with one another — and their various integrated, multi-platform partnerships — in their capacities to contribute to a brand's ability to attain increased levels of engagement, loyalty, and profitability.

ABC-TV: BROADCAST AND THE WEB

Rather than just try and convince advertisers that two touch points were better than one, ABC Television wanted a genuine way to measure multi-platform campaigns and correlate "the blend" or combinations of media used directly for engagement and, more importantly, sales.

While the study results that follow provide actual sales figures for two verticals — Discount Retail and Consumer Packaged Goods — based on exposure to advertising via a digital format, traditional broadcast, and a combination of the two, this same technique can be applied to any product or service category. Where brand values are reinforced, it is absolutely certain that loyalty and profitability follow.

From a 21st century media return-on-investment perspective, it allows TV and digital to present their strengths (beyond appropriate demographics, audience sizes, CPMs, etc.) as they pertain to increased levels of consumer engagement. And for the marketer, this approach can help determine the 'ideal' attributes, benefits, and values (ABVs) that drive loyalty for their type of product or service. This information matched with the evaluation of the media context can provide a marketer with a genuine and leverageable competitive edge in the ongoing struggle for differentiation, increased sales, and market share.

A BRIEF RECAP OF THE METHODOLOGY

The Brand Keys algorithm is a combination of psychological assessments – to provide emotional measures – and a series of higher-order statistical analyses, which provides the rational input. This combination of emotional and rational assessments not only identifies the four drivers of loyalty and engagement for any B2B or B2C category, but also identifies how consumers – again, on a rational *and* emotional basis – see the category attributes, benefits, and values (ABV) as coming together to form the components of the loyalty and engagement drivers. The causal path analysis allows us to calculate the individual percent-contribution each ABV makes to the driver, and therefore, loyalty, engagement, and profitability.

Respondents evaluate category ABVs for importance, with these assessments used as input for a factor analysis, and regression and causal path analyses. This allows us to define the category drivers entirely from a consumer perspective. A weighted average of the brand's assessment — that is, as it measures up to the consumer's conception of the Ideal — is used as a baseline measure for the brand as a stand-alone entity.

Utilizing this same approach, the brand is then measured within the context of various media opportunities: Traditional Media, Digital Platforms, and Traditional and Digital combined.

The assessments we use, *i.e.,* the weighted-average of the brand + the media option variable, identify positive (or neutral, or even negative) effects that the marketing opportunity *makes on the brand values.* For comparison purposes, overall, the weighted indices calculated are benchmarked against an index of 100, with plus/minus 5 index points required for a significant difference at the 95 percent confidence level.

But that's just the nuts and bolts of the process. What's more critical to the marketer (or should be) is the fact that where the brand's values are positively enhanced, this represents a real opportunity for the brand and the media. And where brand values are so enhanced, the brand will *always* see associated, positive consumer behavior in the marketplace. Thus, it allows the media — or combinations of media — to differentiate themselves from the competition, ensuring that the brand is the true beneficiary of the media buy.

The ABC research was conducted in three phases: The first was conducted to predictively measure the levels of brand engagement that *should* result from a brand's advertising on ABC TV, ABC.com, and ABC TV + ABC.com. The second examined the brand advertising's subsequent performance on measures of *category-aided ad awareness, overall brand ratings, and top-2 box purchase intent*. And the third measured what *did* happen; the real, in-market behavior of target consumers who had been exposed to the advertising on the individual platforms and on a combined basis.

PHASE ONE: WHAT SHOULD HAPPEN

An online sample of 500 respondents who regularly watched and/or interacted with ABC TV, ABC.com, and/or both ABC TV and ABC.com assessed the following phase one variables for the Mouthwash Category:

- The Ideal Mouthwash,

- The Listerine brand *as a stand-alone entity*, *i.e.,* on the basis of the respondents' current levels of exposure and knowledge of the brand and *not* in the context of any media vehicle,

- A set of appropriate category attributes, benefits, and values,

- And finally, the Listerine brand *within* the context of each of the platforms, *i.e.,* "Listerine advertised on ABC.com," "Listerine advertised on ABC TV," and "Listerine advertised on ABC. com + ABC TV."

The brand stood up to the consumers' Ideal as follows:

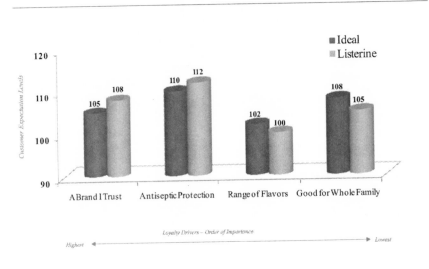

Figure 6.1
Ideal Mouthwash vs. Listerine

Weighted averages of the brands and the brands' advertised on various networks were calculated.

The degree of engagement was calculated based upon whether "advertising on" a particular platform or a combination of platforms significantly increased the levels of brand equity for the brand.

The brand + media option variable was then statistically classified into groups called "High Engagement Media," "Neutral Engagement Media," or "Negative Engagement Media," with, in this instance, results as follows:

Table 6.1
B2ME Scores

High Engagement	
Listerine Advertised on ABC TV and ABC.com	115
Listerine Advertised on ABC.com	112
Listerine Advertised on ABC TV	111
Neutral Engagement	
Listerine	**106**
Negative Engagement	

PHASE TWO: ADVERTISING EFFECTS

Now came the time to determine the actual effects of the Listerine advertising placed on each of the platforms. We used a matched sample of respondents for an online test. The respondents were screened for category consumption and, again, viewership and/or interaction with ABC TV, ABC.com, and a combination of broadcast and digital.

Assessments were gathered for *proven* advertising awareness, brand imagery ratings, and respondents' likelihood to purchase the advertised product. Information was also collected regarding their category purchases over a 3-month period of time, as well as a series of ancillary, category questions.

Based on the findings, it was determined that consumers who saw the commercials on a combined ABC TV + ABC.com effort produced higher levels of advertising awareness, more, positive brand imagery, and higher top-2 box purchase intent than those consumers who saw the commercial on either ABC TV or ABC.com separately. But was that just an outcome of the "more-is-better" theory? The answer would be found in examining consumers' real market behaviors.

PHASE THREE: WHAT DID HAPPEN

The analysis of the respondents' reported purchases confirmed the results observed in phase one of the study, *i.e.*, that actual, in-market behavior among consumers exposed to the advertising via a blend of platforms better reinforced the advertised brand's values. It also produced more, positive brand and market effects, thus highly correlating with the predictive measures from phase one.

Table 6.2
Actual In-Market Behavior and Sales

	B2ME Score	Category Aided Ad Awareness	Brand Imagery (1-7)	Top-2 Box Purchase Intent	Average # Purchased over 6-month period
ABC TV Viewers	111	85%	5.9	52%	3
ABC.com Visitors	112	83%	5.7	50%	3
ABC TV & ABC.com	115	91%	6.2	60%	4
Correlations		0.88	0.79	0.90	0.97

TARGET

For the Discount Retail category, a similar test was conducted for Target, with similar results; the blended media approach (Broadcast + Digital) provided higher levels of engagement than either of the platforms individually.

Table 6.3
B2ME Assessments for Target

High Engagement	
Target Advertised on ABC TV and ABC.com	134
Target Advertised on ABC TV	132
Neutral Engagement	
Target Advertised on ABC.com	124
Target	**120**
Low Engagement	

Again, correlations with the predictive engagement metrics were extraordinarily high:

- Awareness: 0.98

- Brand imagery: 0.94

- Purchase intent: 0.55

- Average 30-day purchases: 0.94

- Average spend: 0.77

In fact, if you calculate average total spend (Average Number of Visits multiplied by Average Spend) it turns out that consumers exposed to the combination of broadcast and digital spent 51 percent *more* than those exposed to the advertising on the digital platform only.

Table 6.4
Actual In-Market Behavior & Sales

	B2ME Score	Category Aided Ad Awareness	Brand Imagery (1-7)	Top-2 Box Purchase Intent	Average # Visits over 30-day period	Average Spend	Average Total Spend
ABC TV Viewers	132	65%	5.8	40%	3	$23.66	$70.98
ABC.com Visitors	124	58%	5.6	36%	3	$23.12	$69.36
ABC TV & ABC.com	134	65%	6.0	37%	4	$26.15	$104.60
Correlations		0.98	0.94	0.55	0.94	0.77	

ADDED, ADDED-VALUE

The High, Neutral, and Negative engagement numbers provide an overall brand + media predictive roadmap that leads to optimum marketing and media opportunities.

It tells you what happenes when you combine media formats. But using this approach also allows marketers and strategic planners to *leverage* real brand and media values by identifying the actual strategic brand effects that can be created by combining platforms.

As one might expect, results from a similar exercise for a competing mouthwash produced — for a different brand with different values — different results. Engagement is, after all, brand specific.

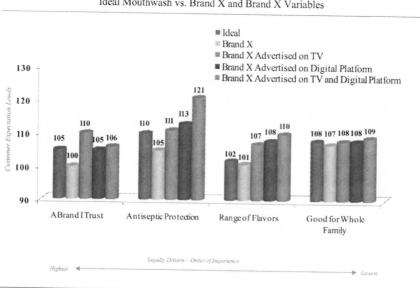

Figure 6.2
Ideal Mouthwash vs. Brand X and Brand X Variables

From the perspective of the consumers' Ideal, Brand X requires significant strategic help on the first, most-important driver, *A Brand I Trust*, and also on the second most-important driver, *Antiseptic Protection*.

Assuming an actual strategy and reasonable creative, addressing the driver *A Brand I Trust* is most economically facilitated by advertising on TV alone, not on a Digital platform and not on a combination of broadcast and digital. Broadcast is the medium where Brand X's values are best reinforced on that driver.

On the other hand, were Brand X to address the issue regarding *Antiseptic Protection*, while TV alone and Digital alone both bring up brand values to just over the expectations for the Ideal, a *combination* of TV and Digital does a far better job engaging consumers on that particular driver and, as we have seen, is likely to engender better behavior and sales in the marketplace.

REAL-WORLD RESULTS AND REAL-WORLD PROFITS

The engagement methodology that fuses emotional and rational elements always provides a predictive way for a marketer to determine if their marketing, branding, or advertising efforts have resulted in increased (or decreased) levels of brand equity. And yes, *how* marketers reach their target audiences has taken on new import, but these same metrics can identify how media — or combinations or blends of media — can best contribute to brand engagement and sales efforts.

Not only do engagement assessments benefit the advertiser, but they can be used by the individual media touch point "brands" and information and entertainment venues to better position, differentiate, and market themselves in an increasingly complex environment.

The high correspondence between engagement assessments and the resultant attitudinal and, *more importantly,* behavioral effects in the marketplace conclusively prove that it is eminently possible to predictively measure which combinations of media venues can better engage an audience.

And that seems to us to be a significantly advantageous position for the media, the media planners, and the brand.

THE KEYHOLE:
PEEKING AT 21ST CENTURY BRANDS:

July 12, 2007

WHAT ENGAGES A WEBSITE VISITOR MOST?

Nielsen/Net Ratings just announced that it now measures website popularity by how much time users spend on sites, rather than how many pages they view. The new measure overturns their previous rankings, so now Yahoo and AOL lead the traditional "winner," Google.

We view this as a particularly idiosyncratic shift because it seems far less to do with actually measuring engagement and much more a reaction to technological changes within the medium itself.

Because websites now incorporate online video, streaming data, and self-refreshing page content, it makes "page views" somewhat superfluous, so you need to change. Measuring total "time spent" is certainly infinitely easier, and is a seductive measure, but it doesn't really provide any real measure of users' "engagement" with the sites.

In a more complex media environment, with more complex (and clever) consumers, it's worth remembering that there is a difference between something being "popular" and something being "engaging." The Super Bowl is extraordinarily popular, but as history has proven, not all advertisers achieve equivalent levels of engagement just because they place their ads on it! Consumers might spend 15 minutes on YouTube, and 30 seconds on Google, but the *raison d'être* for the visit is entirely different (as are the values and expectations that will — or will not — engage the consumer) and, therefore, the engagement "yardstick" you rely upon must also be different. On the web one size does not fit all. That approach may be simple, but it's not precise.

Brand Keys defines engagement as *"the consequence of a marketing or communication effort that results in an increased level of brand equity for the product or service,"* and a variety of validity tests and independent, professional reviews have proven the efficacy and in-market legitimacy and utility of this definition, so the use of the term as Nielsen defined it surprised us.

On the basis of our *Customer Loyalty Engagement Index* we identified the following engagement rankings for the following search sites we monitor:

1. Google.com/Yahoo.com (tie)

2. Netscape.com
3. MSN.com
4. AOL.com
5. AltaVista.com/HotBot.com (tie)
6. Lycos.com
7. Excite.com
8. AskJeeves.com
9. NorthernLight.com

And, given the high correlation between these engagement measures and positive consumer behavior, to a certain degree our approach and measures obviate the "time spent" variable anyway.

To be sure, the "time spent" measure has been exceptionally useful when one is talking about media *allocation,* but as conventional studies of traditional and new media have proven, there is little correlation with "time spent" and real engagement. You can call a Chihuahua a "Greyhound," but it doesn't make it so!

The Brand Keys definition of "engagement" takes into account that websites exist within different competitive landscapes, albeit digital ones. You must examine social networking sites in a vastly different manner than you do search sites. The drivers and values for them are not only different but are often divergent. You really can't compare

MySpace with Google just because they both happen to be sites on the World Wide Web.

Sheryl Draizen of the *Interactive Advertising Bureau* has noted that Nielsen's engagement methodology isn't definitive and that there are other methods to explore. We agree. Nielsen's approach is simple. But simplicity should not be the goal. Simplicity is the by-product of a good idea and modest expectations. These days both marketers and consumers expect more!

1 year, 1 month, and 2 weeks later. . .
Ezine @rticles reported that older traditional measures of website success like Google PageRank and sheer traffic are becoming less meaningful in the current web environment. Business people are now demanding more as marketing professionals have gotten more web-savvy and are looking for more predictive and behavioral analytic tools.

7

The Unreasonable Consumer And Trusting Emotional Trends

The individual choice of garnishment of a burger can be an important point to the consumer in this day when individualism is an increasingly important thing to people.

Donald N. Smith, president of Burger King

Nobel Prize winner Niels Bohr once noted that "prediction is very difficult, especially about the future." Most of the time, real trends come upon us very quickly because their foundations tend to have their roots in emotion and not the rational side of either the consumer or the category. That is due to the very nature of trends themselves. Tsunami-like when obvious but beginning somewhere on the ocean floor, by the time most marketers see trends they experience only their leveling force, unable to ride the wave. They come too quick, and every brand is swept along in a me-too undifferentiated swirl.

It's impossible to over-sell the importance to marketers of having predictive metrics. Add to that, predictive metrics that *measure emotion* — without using the direct question that is so often ineffective — and brands have a chance of being the next big thing 12 to 18 months in advance of a trend becoming discernable to just anyone in the marketplace.

There are, of course, trends that have their roots in reason, but you don't need to dig very far to find an emotional component far more powerful than the technology or the feature. Take, for example, the camera that is now a fundamental and expected part of your cell or smart phone. There was a time not long ago when mobile phones didn't have a camera in them. They got there because Sanyo had the chip in their labs. The camera was included in the hope of providing the brand with a degree of rational product differentiation at a time when cell phones were all pretty much alike — not because there were consumers walking around saying, "boy, you know what my cell phone really needs? A camera. Wouldn't that be cool!?"

Try buying a phone today *without* a camera in it. It's a given. Being able to add visuals to the most intimate communication medium people use — the phone — created an emotional response in the marketplace that was undeniable.

With the articulation of attributes, benefits, and values (ABVs) that are truly important, a brand can focus its resources to amazing market results — as demonstrated by our work with Mobil. Mobil asked Brand Keys to assist in solving a strategic brand management challenge. Despite extensive franchise renovations to existing properties, *i.e.,* complete beverage/snack centers, self-serve pumps, covered islands, indoor-entry restrooms, etc., Mobil could not increase market share against rivals, who were doing the same.

The Brand Keys consumer research approach was able to identify the key attribute or value that would *truly* drive the consumers' future purchase in the category — because it made a high contribution to engagement. The insight? The attribute identified as key was *"Getting in and out of the station quickly."* The rest is brand strategy and marketing program history. The Mobil "Speedpass®" was born, offering differentiation to Mobil in the marketplace of that time — using RFID technology to meet an emotional consumer need: give me more time. It's been reported that this differentiating strategy resulted in an extra tank a month among Mobil Speedpass customers.

But what about when consumers are not able to articulate their needs as clearly? Then, more than ever, the brand needs metrics that track where categories are *going,* not where they have been.

One calendar quarter, our predictive metrics study for Chrysler revealed that the *"Accessibility"* customer loyalty driver had significantly increased its impact on the consumer in the mini-van category. This kind of movement reveals a true marketplace shift in needs and expectations of consumers, and recognition of it can be like striking gold for a brand.

The result? Chrysler understood the value of this *predictive* data. It quickly determined that adding a fourth van door would best reinforce this changing customer value. Up to this point, all vans had two front doors and one side door.

The 4-door van was an unqualified success, and it took the competition *two to three years* to catch up.

We tell these stories because they illustrate why it is so important for marketers to have data that sees trends coming. While Samsung's forty-three day exclusive window for the camera phone was not enough to garner long-term meaningful differentiation or market share, you can own emotional trends *if* you lay claim to them before your competition. Remember Rosser Reeves' *USP*, the *Unique Selling Proposition*? That applies to emotional values too. Maybe better than rational ones.

We have already demonstrated — via various discussions regarding real loyalty and engagement output — that these metrics can be used as an early warning system for trends. Waiting for shifts in category and customer values to manifest as a cultural phenomenon — what Malcolm Gladwell called "the tipping point" — means that it's often too late to take advantage of them from a marketing standpoint. And, even when the divinations and pronouncements of trend watchers are right, marketers do not generally know upon *which aspect* of the trend to focus, let alone know if they are making investments too late. Where to look, who to follow?

Well, to paraphrase Ludwig Mies van der Rohe, trend details are in the drivers. Trends can reveal themselves in the way category drivers are configured. How can a shift in how consumers view a category be used to a brand's advantage? In some cases, the very nature of the attributes, benefits, and values that form the components of the drivers themselves change, which should give you a trend-sighting well ahead of your tracking study. We have seen this in numerous categories like quick-service dining, when "health" showed up as force in the category, or when "green" materials came, seemingly, out of nowhere in the athletic shoe category.

The percent-contribution that individual components make to engagement and loyalty change, and when they increase, that's usually the tip of a coming trend. Think of it as a "Tipping Point Early Warning System." If you know that *before* the competition, you get more than a forty-three day lead in consumers' hearts and minds, as well as in the marketplace. Measuring real consumer expectations works too. The growing gap between expectations and delivery is the very definition of consumer disengagement and disloyalty and a potential loss of equity for brands. Real loyalty and engagement metrics provide all these indicators.

WHAT HAVE YOU DONE FOR ME LATELY?

The expectations of today's "bionic" consumers are perhaps best captured in British writer George Bernard Shaw's quotation, "The reasonable man adapts himself to the world. The unreasonable one persists in customizing the world to himself and his values." And you really don't have to look too closely at the marketplace to concede that today's consumers expect everything. Woe unto the product or service that can't deliver on those expectations ahead of the competition! That's where identifying real trends can be very useful. But you have to know how.

Trend sighting can only come from authentic consumer-generated analyses. By examining the predictive, leading-indicator changes in the drivers and the value components that comprise them in our annual *Customer Loyalty Engagement Index,* we found that the average percent-of-contribution that "customization" makes to product and service engagement, adoption, loyalty, and profitability is currently 18 percent. That's nearly five times what the value was when we first measured it in 1997. Back then it was only four percent, and the climb has been constant and seemingly without a ceiling!

Figure 7.1
Growth of Customization Value
(1997-2008)

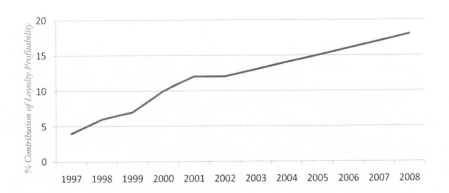

Examples reveal themselves everywhere. You can go online and design your own running shoes right down to the color of the shoelaces or the location (and color) of the logo version you prefer. Or you can customize your new automobile. Choice of color (exterior and interior) is passé as a differentiator; it's a given. Today you can customize the interior, right down to the high-tech, MP3, GPS, voice-controlled options you so desire, or the design of the hubcaps. Catalogs allow for women to virtually customize their bathing suits for size, style, and color.

Or you can put your child's graduation photo or a picture of Fluffy the family cat on your credit card, while you select the APR you deign to be charged, *and* select the time of month you want your statement to be sent, by mail or electronically. You can also pick from any of the 87,000 customized coffee combinations currently available. A half double decaffeinated half-caf vanilla latte with a twist of lemon and no foam may have been funny in the 1991 movie, *L.A. Story,* but today it's pretty much the price of entry into the coffee category. Think about how you customize your computer right down to the screensaver photo of your trip to the Great Barrier Reef. How many ways do you customize your computer or PDA for the time of day it automatically collects mail or updates programs or reminds you of meetings or birthdays and anniversaries? Let us count the ways.

Think about your cell phone and how you customize what it looks like, what it sounds like, and what you can do with it. And if you want bottom-line proof as to those kinds of engagement opportunities, you only have to look at LG Electronics® and their 54 percent growth in shipments of cellular phones in the first quarter of 2008. That's nearly four times the 14 percent average for the industry and it was due primarily to the ability to offer phones with 5-megapixel cameras and software that allows users to create their own music videos. And if you're looking for a very personal example, Revlon Custom Creations™ foundation makeup now comes in a bottle with an adjustable dial that offers five settings so that consumers can fine-tune shades customized for their own skin tones. Even hotels will customize your room from the softness (or hardness) of the mattress to the kind of pillow *you* prefer. Yes, it all seems like it's in the details, but these are the kinds of details that most consumers expect and take for granted today. They are the aspects of differentiation that marketers and brands can't ignore. The customization aspects of these products and services are *expected,* and those expectations aren't lessening. If the trends continue, customization will be the largest individual contributor to differentiation for the next decade.

In the 2008 Brand Keys *Customer Loyalty Engagement Index,* the Top-10 categories where customization has become one of the largest brand differentiators are:

1. Coffee Providers
2. Automobiles
3. Athletic Footwear
4. Online
5. Wireless

6. Cell Phones
7. Hotels
8. Restaurants
9. Parcel Delivery
10. Clothing Catalogs

And those are only the Top-10. But take a look at the differences between the categories. The percent-contribution that customization makes not only differs from category-to-category, but also differs in the way in which it drives differentiation, engagement, loyalty, and certainly profitability.

Table 7.1
"Customization" Contribution By Top-10 Categories

Coffee Providers	Automotive	Athletic Footwear	On-Line	Wireless
35%	24%	22%	20%	20%

Cell Phones	Hotels	Restaurants	Parcel Delivery	Clothing Catalogs
18%	15%	13%	10%	9%

What most marketers need to do is to take a long hard look at their categories. If they move beyond the standard, tracking peek at the marketplace, they'll discover that most of the products and services with whom they compete *are* providing perfectly acceptable levels of primacy of product or service. And that their customers are perfectly "satisfied" with what they're getting. The question — on both a loudly articulated *and* a silently unarticulated basis — being asked by the consumer today is, "What have you done for *ME* lately?" Which is a really, really important question when consumers are going to judge you — not with a sliced 'n diced satisfaction award — but with their wallets and pocketbooks.

OK, "What have you done for me lately?" may, at first blush, seem like a perfectly unreasonable question. But then, to finish Mr. Shaw's quotation, brands may find that "all progress and profitability, therefore, depends on unreasonable people." And the questions they ask of us. To be successful you need to anticipate the questions and have answers at the ready, and real engagement measures can help you be prepared for when consumer demands show up at your brand's doorstep.

LOVE ALL, TRUST A FEW

That subhead was written by William Shakespeare in *All's Well That Ends Well*. But it comes to mind every time we are asked about the cornucopia of media options that have become part of the unfortunate trend "my-competitor-is-using-(FILL IN THE MEDIUM)-so-I-ought-to-too." What was once novelty, now seems necessary, or so say some marketers. Their conversion to believers seems to have been driven mostly by "the trend" that the platform or opportunity is A) available, and B) seems to be inserting itself into the lives of more and more consumers, some of which might actually be among their target audience.

For example, in August 2008 a new advertising medium was announced to the marketing world with great fanfare. The initiators of this new platform, convinced that the marketing world was hungering for yet another communication touch point, proclaimed that it intended to engage consumers and reach their minds and hearts through their stomachs!

The medium was to be made up of a national network of convenience stores, sandwich shops, snack bars, cafes, and delicatessens. Within this new network, food purveyors contractually agreed to replace the plain waxed paper they had previously used to wrap sandwiches and snacks with a proprietary, branded paper. Advertisers could then have breakfast, lunch, dinner, and snack sandwiches wrapped with branding that "reached their target audiences," who were apparently starving for yet another commercial message thrust into their private moments, in this case, mealtimes.

Although this all sounds very creative, engagement levels may be uncertain. One can only wonder if the wrapping paper itself will become just part of the background. The one thing for absolutely certain is that the marketer will know for sure where their brand, their logo, and their carefully crafted communications are ultimately going to end up!

But perhaps more important than having your brand tossed into the great rubbish bin of desktop meals, there is the very real question of whether consumers will actually *trust* a message that smells of limburger and upon which the spattered detritus of their morning bacon and egg sandwich, lunchtime sloppy Joe, or snack-sized slab of pepperoni pizza rests. Because it isn't attention or awareness that's the issue, it's whether the consumer will trust the medium itself.

Well, for the moment let's look at the trend of trust and the media as a facilitator of trust. As commoditization has crept closer and closer to all products and services, including actual brands, marketers have come to assess media on the basis of values like "trust." It's become a kind of universal value, but critical nonetheless.

In Chapter Five we outlined the theory that some media assessment companies have put forward: if the medium is regarded as "trustworthy," your brand will too if you advertise in that most "trustworthy" of venues. And the question of whether and to what degree your brand needs a media-infused dose of "trust" notwithstanding, the approach generally treats all media as having equal measures of "trust" — or at least as much as it's rated on a 1-to-5 trustworthiness scale — for all categories.

While this is the line of reasoning that is put forward for the model, this just isn't the case no matter how much promotion and sales-speak is put behind the archetype. One category is vastly different than another category. Brands are different from one another, or should be. And the degree to which media platforms are imbued with, for example, "trust," will vary from category-to-category and platform-to-platform.

Doubt us? What follows is an assessment of fourteen categories, from bar soap to banks, from auto to fast food, and the degree to which eight different media platforms — everything from Cable to Online — are actually imbued with the value "trust."

Table 7.2
Percent-Contribution of "Trust" By Media Type

	TV (Broadcast)	TV (Cable)	Radio	Newspapers	Magazines	Direct Mail	Outdoor	Online
Allergy (Rx)	20	20	5	9	11	13	2	12
Automotive	18	16	4	10	20	9	5	22
Banking	20	18	12	8	10	18	4	10
Bar Soap	20	20	12	16	18	10	6	6
Computers	12	14	2	12	5	10	4	16
Cookies	18	19	10	14	18	8	2	5
Credit Cards	22	20	12	10	10	13	1	15
Department Stores	18	14	20	28	16	20	2	13
Discount Stores	22	21	15	20	13	19	4	10
Insurance	18	16	8	16	12	10	1	15
Mouthwash	10	10	5	6	9	9	1	10
OTC Pain Relievers	20	20	11	17	15	10	3	11
Quick Serve Restaurants	18	20	8	16	12	10	4	4
Wireless	14	12	2	13	10	10	2	16

Note the ranges that might be available to you, depending upon the category in which you compete. Credit cards? Twenty-two percent on Broadcast TV, but only one percent for Outdoor. And please don't say, "Oh, well, you know. . ." because the reality is that they were all considered, are all used, and depending upon how they've been positioned by the advertising agency or media planners, not only all deemed appropriate but all, somehow, above average. But this is clearly *not* the case. Some media platforms will work harder for some categories than others — for precisely the same value, but not for the same costs or outcomes.

So let us listen to Shakespeare and "love all, trust a few." But if you use engagement assessments to identify trends, you'll be able to complete the quote and "do wrong to none," — especially to your brand.

THE KEYHOLE:
PEEKING AT 21ST CENTURY BRANDS:

July 12, 2007

ILLEGALLY BLONDE

As more and more "brands" lose meaning and find themselves turning into "Category Placeholders," more and more turn to celebrities to provide that missing daub of differentiation. So what happens when the celebrities the brands rely upon go bad?

As the old ad adage went, since "blondes have more fun," what of the most recent celebrity trio to go bad, Paris Hilton, Lindsay Lohan, and Nicole Richie, all involved in some combination of alcohol and/or drug DUI/probation violation?

Loyalty and engagement research have identified four patterns of customer response when good brands do bad things:

1. The more heavily the celebrity is associated with the brand, the more devastating the effects.
2. Brands who use celebrities' names only to, for example, label or franchise a product will see less damage.

3. The public is kinder to male celebrities than they are to women.

4. Brands that have no celebrity association will — in bad times — see about half the negative effects compared to a celebrity-associated brand.

And how do our celebrities feel about all this? Well, Paris Hilton said, "I feel that I was treated unfairly. . . I don't deserve this."

Strangely, brands that didn't vet their celebrities, feel the same way!

1 year and 10 months later. . .

Certain Fact: There is actually a listing for "celebrity spokespersons" on myspace job$.

8

FUTURE PROFITS

Frontier Rube: Is this a game of chance?
W.C. Fields: Not the way I do it!

My Little Chickadee

It's been said that all evidence shows that God was actually a gambler. That the universe is really just a great casino, where dice are thrown, slot machine handles are pulled, and roulette wheels spin on every occasion and for every event. And, over a large number of bets, the odds even out, so mathematicians and scientists are able to make predictions.

But marketing is different; brands and marketing — and particularly the consumers that brands want to attract and about whom marketing mostly concerns itself — don't always abide by the laws of the physical universe. It doesn't matter if it's B2B or B2C you're talking about, consumers are smarter about categories and brands than any other time in marketing history and exponentially more elusive than ever before. That's when having loyalty and engagement metrics that measure the consumer universe come in handy. About that you can be certain.

Properly configured, loyalty and engagement assessments can measure the direction and velocity of future consumer values, often 12 to 18 months in advance. And they can be applied to brands, markets, media, and creative with an accuracy that would get you barred from a Las Vegas casino.

They can be used to identify category drivers and individual attributes, benefits, and values (ABVs) that can differentiate you from your competition and emotionally bond consumers to your brand. You can take what has become an extraordinarily complex media ecology and bring some calming structure and predictive insights to what appears to the naked eye — and a good deal of cross-media consumption gobbledygook — to be chaos. You can measure awareness all you want but brands who do not meaningfully engage with consumers are certain to become "Category Placeholders."

In the absence of your brand having obtained real engagement and loyalty metrics, we can recommend creating a Brand Upward Yield Score®, also known as a BUY Score. While not providing leading-indicator loyalty and engagement-based assessments, it can provide you with a positive-indicator of brand success (or failure) that can be used to identify relative ROI.

The BUY Score is an aggregate assessment of four, key brand measures including:

1. Brand image,
2. Likelihood to purchase,

3. An indication of how much they like the brand, and

4. Likelihood to recommend to a friend or colleague.

Each of the four BUY Score measures is rated on a one-to-ten scale, where one is low and ten is high. For those of you familiar with the Net Promoter™ score, which attempts to measure the talk-value generated by a brand, the BUY Score includes that aspect but also incorporates three other critical measures — giving the marketer a score four times as powerful as the Net Promoter.

The total of the ratings on the four scales is then multiplied by 2.5. Rated outside the context of advertising or media or another marketing scenario, the resultant number represents the brand's positive-indicator benchmark. It is then possible to use that benchmark to calculate pre-post ratios, not unlike the traditional Price/Earnings Ratios, with an equation that looks like this:

$$\text{BUY Score} = \frac{\text{Brand Increase/Decrease After Initiative}}{\text{Brand Score Before Initiative}}$$

So, if your Brand BUY Score benchmark is 70, and you test initiative A and initiative B, and initiative A results in a brand evaluation of 80, your BUY Score equation would look like this:

$$\text{BUY Score} = \frac{10}{70} = 14\%$$

On the other hand, suppose initiative B resulted in brand evaluation of 92, your BUY Score would then look like this:

$$\text{BUY Score} = \frac{22}{70} = 31\%$$

Which ROI would you like to see?

In the interest of fair disclosure and an unwillingness to disappoint our readers, we remind you that this is merely a *positive-indicator* assessment. Unlike real loyalty and engagement-based measures these do not merely "translate" into "Initiative B will produce 31% return on the effort." Nor does it offer the granularity a brand needs to develop nuanced strategy and communications efforts. Would that it were that easy.

But the BUY Score can be built into your marketing models and it can provide a comparative option for assessing market, media, and communication effects.

As brands become more and more enamored with and enmeshed in "new" media like social networking, buzz, and messages beamed into consumers' living rooms from outer space, marketers need to ensure that their brands actually stand for something in the mind of the consumer. Media planning is necessary and sometimes even engaging, but those who rely on flavorof-the-week tactics will find that they are forcing their consumers down pathways where ultimately only price will differentiate their well-known products from the competition. And that is a risky situation! So companies will have to move from talking about brand engagement to actually doing something about it.

Rating numbers, breakthrough numbers, click-through rates, approval ratings, ethnographics, psychographics, household demographics, TV households, rating points, radio ratings, word-of-mouth gossip, blog bluster, buzz hearsay, image ratings, satisfaction ratings, tracking numbers, saliency levels, and a mélange of metrics and metrix all provide input. Like Alan Sherman's parody song, "promise miracles, magic and hope but somehow it always turns out to be soap," or, in this case, data. Marketers do not suffer from a lack of data; they suffer from a lack of predictive insights! One needs 20:20 foresight, not hindsight.

Voltaire noted, "Indeed, history is nothing more than a tableau of crimes and misfortunes," or perhaps, in this case, just the crime of mismarketing. Working with legacy measures and lagging-indicators does not allow one to prepare for what's coming at them at faster and faster velocities.

FUTURE CERTAINTIES

Engagement is not a fad. It is not going away and it is the only proven measure that will predict what *will* happen to your brand in the marketplace. It's been proven that real engagement is the outcome of any marketing or media initiative that substantively improves a brand's equity. And, no matter what branded and trademarked name your agency has attached to it, real "brand equity" is the degree to which a brand is seen to meet — or even exceed — consumers' expectations for the category in which it competes. It doesn't matter what image you attach. Image is just the creative shell that encases the resonating and differentiating values that make you a brand. This is getting harder and harder to measure using models that had already lost their efficacy in 1985. And when you combine that with the power of today's "bionic" consumers, born hot-wired into the Internet with an iPod in one hand and a TiVo or Nintendo Wii® controller in the other, engaging them will be the only way of guaranteeing loyalty and profitability.

Having examined these measures in our *Customer Loyalty Engagement Index*, we are able to identify values and trends, and offer up some final thoughts that we are certain will have direct consequences to the success — or failure — of the efficacy of your brand's current marketing efforts, and your future profits.

CUSTOMIZATION

In August 2008, the Gap, and who had just announced a negative 11 percent same-store sales figure, opted to leverage a trend we identified with our metrics quite some time ago, and discussed previously in this book: customization. Consumers' heightened feelings of control about virtually every aspect of their lives — but particularly where they shop and what they buy — and a response to the loss of "brandness" in virtually everything, revealed itself in the desire for more customized stuff.

As we mentioned in Chapter 7, the average percent-contribution "customization" makes to product and service engagement, adoption, and loyalty is currently 18 percent, nearly five times what the value was when we first measured it in 1997. The climb has been constant and seemingly without a ceiling. And it has been leverageable for those who do it right, and apparently it only just showed up on the Gap's research radar.

Well, better late than never, we suppose. But the real question is, will a beautiful set of black and white photographs featuring a diverse group of actors and would-be style makers largely unknown to many consumers communicate customization? How many of them do you know? (Ginnifer Goodwin, Edgar Ramirez, Catalina Sandino Moreno, Melvil Poupaud, Clemence Poesy, Joe Anderson, Georgina Chapman, Julia Restoin Roitfeld, Scott Schuman, Leigh Lezark, Max Lugavere, and Jason Silva.) Can each of them, wearing Gap clothes in unique ways (according to the Gap), be seen as authentic "customization" or is it just "celebrity spokespersoning?" And if the Gap campaign strikes you as a kind of updated 1950's "mix n' match," pearls and sweater set approach and not customization as it manifests itself in the category, you're not wrong.

Want the 21st century version? Go to Nike's or adidas' online site and create a customized pair of shoes for yourself. Or design the car of your dreams on the Mini site. Or customize your membership application for Fred's

Breakfast, and you'll have a sense of the benchmark consumers are using when it comes to "customization."

GREEN

Just talking about how concerned a brand is about the environmental arena won't be an option in the coming years. The environment is making itself felt in what actually drives categories and in the value upon which brand equities will rest. What used to be the "Materials and Manufacturing" driver in the athletic shoe category now includes "Carbon Footprinting," and right now only Nike seems to be the brand doing anything about it. Nike has publicized its plan to reduced greenhouse gasses and trim factory inefficiencies by making cleaner, more sustainable designs in Nike's own lab, to be completed by 2011. Brands and holding companies will have to position their offerings in ways that meaningfully support a sustainable future, because this is an engagement value that can be leveraged only by brands that can do it believably.

And remember how we told you that neither the categories nor the consumers were carved in stone? Consumer knowledge and expectations grow exponentially. And as the number of companies trying to co-opt the environmental movement for their products and services grows, so too will the number of skeptical, "bionic" consumers. They've heard these promises before, and in the face of business-as-usual advertising puffery, will demand authenticity.

Toyota, which used to be known for its "reliability" still is, but it also pretty much owns "hybrid" as a differentiating value. Yes, other car manufacturers make hybrids, but — to paraphrase Will Rogers — saying it, doing it, and *owning it*, are three vastly different things. "Environmental Responsibility" came on strong as a driver of loyalty in the automobile category. No longer the "old green" of a highly-altruistic fringe group, it is inexorably linked to "fuel efficiency," and mainstream consumers are demanding that brands respond with both an environmental and financially sound product.

COST/VALUE

Every day the headlines are there to remind us that the slowing US economy is having ripple effects throughout the business world. While it is tempting to look at any category and blame slowing sales on harder times, that is not always the case. Cost-centric drivers moved up in only 13 of the 57 categories we track — demonstrating that generalizations about the economy's impact don't hold; some categories are seeing that rise in importance, but many are not. This speaks to the necessity of a category-based perspective when thinking of how consumers shop.

Some categories that are seeing price/value become more important are bottled water, cell phones, energy providers, and diapers — all "can't live without" items where consumers have seen increasing brand proliferation with little distinction. However, price and value rarely move alone. In the case of bottled water, this dovetails with another trend we just discussed: green. Many consumers have not only done the math on what they spend on something that comes out of their faucet for free, but are increasingly alarmed by the thought of empty bottles adding to already-cluttered landfills. This suggests that the blue ribbon of profits may go to the brand that can address both these issues. Some water brands have already responded with "green" bottling that is more environmentally friendly.

HEALTHY CHOICES

The quick-service restaurant category has seen "health" become increasingly important, and this will likely continue to rise. However, brands will need to respond with the variety and selection that consumers have come to expect, offering healthy alternatives that satisfy.

The pizza category — surely one of the most cluttered and hotly-contested categories in the marketplace — continues to show a similar trend. Chains that have been slow to respond to the consumer's demand for "the extras," beyond the pie, will continue to suffer. Chains who do not learn how to believably migrate from "fast food" to "real meals" will find themselves marginalized.

CUSTOMER SERVICE

To those who thought customer service dead in the online age, think again — when it comes to certain categories, that is.

Not surprisingly, consumers voiced their opinions in our data long before the press began to chronicle the demise of airline service. The airlines that have made service a priority — Southwest and JetBlue — share the top spot for customer loyalty and engagement. This will continue to be a differentiator for airlines, and those that can do it while offering a reasonable price will lead the market.

When it comes to service stations, offering customers a "physical plant" where they can use a clean restroom, feel safe under bright lighting, and duck in for a gallon of milk, will offer the service that customers are looking for. However, while very important, this is not where a station will differentiate. A good physical plant is now cost-of-entry in the category. To differentiate, stations will need to find ways to offer the customer a reward for their loyalty in this price-challenged market. And not an empty loyalty card program with meaningless points, but a program with a true customer benefit.

SIMPLIFICATION

In the over-committed world, consumers are searching for simplification. In some categories this is showing up strong, such as cell-phone plans, search engines, and laundry detergent. Who has not looked at switching cellular carriers and audibly sighed at the task of comparing one complicated plan to another? Search engines come into our experience often when we need something quickly and want it fast — not to be sent to page one of 480,000. And who really wants to deal with niche laundry products when you're trying to get it done and still have some part of Saturday to yourself?

Simplification is also showing up as a driver in online travel sites. Makes sense, yet as the competition has heated up they continue to compete on price, and not what the consumer will trade some dollars for — an uncomplicated experience.

SHOPPING EXPERIENCE

From Main Street discounters to Madison Avenue boutiques, shoppers continue to be driven by a strong desire for store experience. No matter what the level of retail, customers want to enter more than just a building when they shop. They want to *feel* different, not just *be* somewhere different. The popular term "retail therapy" has its roots in a very real experience that consumers have when they shop, or at least that they *can* have. A positive shopping experience can turn the chore of shopping from all work into all play — as Nordstrom's customers have repeatedly and exuberantly exclaimed about their stores. There is no end of loyalty in sight for the brand that can satisfy consumers craving for store experience.

WITH GREAT CERTAINTY

Consumer expectations will continue to grow. Brands are only barely keeping up now. Expectations remained stable for a short time, but only while consumers were catching their collective breath and adopting — then devouring — the newest of the new technologies and innovations. Smart marketers will absolutely need to identify and capitalize upon unmet expectations.

Values like "customization" and "personalization" will be more and more leveraged via high-tech capabilities to differentiate themselves from their competitors. "Health" and "green," as consciousness is raised and wallets stretched, and "simplification," for already stressed lives, are values that will need watching.

In the absence of actual ownership of these values and outright recognition as such by consumers, marketers will have to rely upon traditional and new media formats and social networking as a way of creating real engagement between them and their target audiences. This is a stop-gap measure, and one that will not build muscular brands that can hold their own. As the proverb goes, "if you continue following the same road you will reach the same destination."

So where is the road to the future leading? The landscape will involve more and more predictive measures that are both innovative and comprehensive. Engagement will flourish when brands can foretell needs and expectations of their audiences and when brand values and communications are actively driving behavior. The trend will be toward anticipation and prediction.

Accommodating these trends will require a paradigm shift on the parts of some companies. But keep in mind that change is the process by which the future invades our lives. And whether you do something about it or not, the future is where you — and your brand — are going to spend the rest of your lives.

For certain.

THE KEYHOLE:
PEEKING AT 21ST CENTURY BRANDS:

March 13, 2006

THINKING ABOUT THE BOX

These days it's obvious that consumer "engagement" is much more than just running an ad on a well-watched TV show. It involves all aspects of marketing a product. That includes package design.

But from a packaging perspective, it's not easy to fruitfully manage all the marketing inputs and mandates that tend to be contributed when a new package is being designed.

Everyone wants something "new," and "leading-edge," and "creative," and something that "pushes the envelope," as it were. It is one of those areas that get a good deal of thought from a shelf-attention generating, visual perspective, but very little about how (or how much) it contributes to consumer engagement.

We recognize that consumer engagement metrics are relatively new to most marketers but they are totally absent from the package design arena. You can't force yourself — visually or otherwise — into consumers' lives, you need to be invited.

And we think that it's fair to say that when it comes to engagement, marketers might be more enthusiastic about encouraging thinking outside the box when there's evidence of any thinking going on inside it.

2 years and 5 months later. . .

In highlights from the AAAA 2008 Account Planning Conference, it was reported that things are very different today. People aren't waiting to hear from advertisers. Brands need to earn the right to be welcomed into consumers' lives.

But, as we hope this book has verified, of that, we've always been certain!

INDEX

ABOUT THE AUTHORS

Robert Passikoff

Dr. Robert Passikoff, Brand Key's founder and president, is a sought-after speaker and thought leader on engagement and loyalty. He has pioneered work in these areas, creating the Brand Keys *Customer Loyalty Engagement Index*, the *Brandweek* Loyalty Leaders List, the Sports Fan Loyalty Index®, and the *Women's Wear Daily* Fashion Brand Engagement Index®. His first best-selling book, *Predicting Market Success,* provided marketers with a 21st century perspective on predictive metrics. In 2001 he introduced Brand-to-Media Engagement metrics, a 21st century media-planning tool that allows advertisers to select the best medium for their advertising, *before* spending their money in addition to identifying cross-media consumption effects that correlate to in-market consumer behavior and sales. In 2007, New York University's communication school declared Dr. Passikoff "the most-quoted brand consultant in the United States." In past lives Dr. Passikoff served as VP, Director of Research for Citibank and SVP, Planning Director for Cato Johnson/Y&R where he created their worldwide "Action Marketing" paradigm. His academic credentials include a Master's Degree in Communications Psychology from Oxford University and a Ph.D. in Psychology from New York University. Robert is currently a contributing editor for *Brandweek* and a columnist for *Chief Marketer* and is a frequent guest commentator for CNN and *MarketWatch*.

Currently he is a Guest Lecturer at Northwestern and Columbia Universities, and an Adjunct Associate Professor at New York University. In 2007, the Advertising Research Foundation presented Dr. Passikoff with their Research Innovator award for the impact of his work on advancing the industry.

Amy Shea

Amy Shea, Brand Key's EVP and Director of Brand Development, has worked with brands for over twenty years, specializing in translating research-based insights into effective brand communications. A published and fellowed poet and writer, Amy helps brands create strategically-based communications informed by a deep understanding of metaphor. She has led teams of copy editors, artists, and designers in aligning both internal and external communications with a brand's identity. Her experience in media sales, media buying, and media creation, as well as a deep background in marketing research combines with her strong creative talents to bring a unique analysis of data within the context of brand-story structure. Previous to her work with Brand Keys, Amy was Vice President and Research Director for Ameritest, where she worked on many top brands, including the global research for IBM. Her work was recognized with IBM in 2003 with the David Ogilvy Excellence Award, taking both the Grand Ogilvy and First in Category for the research conducted on IBM's integrated campaign on infrastructure. Amy has worked with clients across categories — ranging from CPG, to financial services, to retail giants — as well as across media — researching television advertising and programming, newspaper, magazine, direct mail, and packaging. Shea presents on brand development, differentiation, engagement, and the branded entertainment category in the United States, Europe, and Asia on a regular basis. In 2008, Amy Shea was chosen by the Advertising Research Foundation for a Great Minds Award in the Innovation category, to recognize her achievements in advancing the field of research.

Printed in the United States
208956BV00001B/163-213/P